Oasis

Dynamic Intercession

MIKE BICKLE

WORD BOOKS
Nelson Word Ltd
Milton Keynes, England
WORD AUSTRALIA
Kilsyth, Victoria, Australia
WORD COMMUNICATIONS LTD
Vancouver, B.C., Canada
STRUIK CHRISTIAN BOOKS (PTY) LTD
Cape Town, South Africa
CHRISTIAN MARKETING NEW ZEALAND LTD
Havelock North, New Zealand
JENSCO LTD
Hong Kong
JOINT DISTRIBUTORS SINGAPORE –
ALBY COMMERCIAL ENTERPRISES PTE LTD
and
CAMPUS CRUSADE, ASIA LTD
SALVATION BOOK CENTRE
Malaysia

ISBN 0-85009-806-8 (Australia 1-86258-288-2)

Created, designed and typeset by Frontier Publishing International Ltd., BN43 6RE, England. *Reproduced, printed and bound in Great Britain for* Nelson Word Ltd. *by* Bushey Mead Press.

93 94 95 96 / 10 9 8 7 6 5 4 3 2 1

Making the most of the studies ...

Welcome

Welcome to the Oasis study on *Dynamic Intercession*! God often chooses to limit His activity until His people pray. This book underlines the vital importance of intercession, makes practical suggestions regarding how to pray, and helps you to see that your prayers play a key part in establishing God's purposes on earth.

2 days equals 2 months

We suggest that you take two days to cover each study and therefore two months to complete the book. You may feel you want to work through the material more quickly, but if you take your time you are likely to benefit more. We recommend that you use the New International Version of the Bible (post-1983 version). The important thing is not that you finish fast, but that you hear from God *en route*! So aim to learn well and steadily build the teaching into your life.

Respond to the challenge

When Israel was steeped in evil, the Lord was 'astonished that there was no one to intercede' (Isa. 59:16b NASB). Today many nations are wallowing in sin, and God is ever searching for people who will pray.

Mike Bickle provides us with the chance to respond to this challenge. He highlights the brevity of life and the need to be captivated by eternal values. With reference to his own devotional life, he suggests a pattern for intercession which includes worship, meditation on the Word, petition, praying in tongues and silently enjoying the presence of God. He also explains how we can pray corporately for the breakthrough of the Holy Spirit in our nation.

The three sections under the main text relate to the teaching material. You may be asked to consider some aspect of intercession, to write down an answer, or simply to do something practical. The questions and verses of Scripture have been designed to inform you about prayer and to encourage you to engage in it.

Build a storehouse

The Bible says, 'Wise men store up knowledge' (Prov. 10:14), and Jesus underlines this when He calls us to '[bring] good things out of the good stored up in [our] heart' (Luke 6:45).

God wants to encourage and inform you through His Word. That's what the 'Food for thought' section is all about. It gives you the invaluable opportunity to hear direct from God and to store up what He says to you. **Please use a separate notebook** particularly for this section. Not only will it help you to crystallise your thoughts, but it will also be of tremendous reference value in the future.

As you study, refuse to let time pressurise you. Pray that God will speak to you personally and expect Him to do so. You may sometimes find that you're so enthralled by what He says to you that you're looking up many Scriptures which are not even suggested!

Finally, may God bless you richly through this book. Realise afresh how much you can achieve through prayer and respond to the challenge.

6/8/93

❑ STUDY 1

'Remain in me, and I will remain in you. No branch can bear fruit by itself; it must remain in the vine. Neither can you bear fruit unless you remain in me. I am the vine; you are the branches. If a man remains in me and I in him, he will bear much fruit; apart from me you can do nothing' (John 15:4,5).

The kingdom of God is not a matter of eating and drinking, but of righteousness, peace and joy in the Holy Spirit (Rom. 14:17).

Remain in me

Many Christians long for the kind of supernatural anointing that has a profound and lasting impact on others. They no longer want to see individuals asking for help one week and returning with the same problems the next. Rather, they're keen to be channels of God's power, bringing complete transformation to the lives of those to whom they minister.

Jesus wants us not only to bear much fruit, He wants it to last. The fruit is 'righteousness, peace and joy in the Holy Spirit'. Jesus wants us to affect others in such a way that these qualities spring up in their lives and remain in them — even in the midst of extreme pressure and injustice. How can we have this sort of powerful impact? Only through an intimate relationship with Him.

All the other religions of the world follow moral precepts. But Christians have been called into fellowship with God's Son, a living Person who interacts with His people. He invites us to draw near to Him and promises that if we do, He will draw near to us. Jesus' invitations are also commands, but none of them is given without the understanding of

▩ To assess

Write down 5 qualities of an intimate relationship, e.g. trust.

Trust, openness, security, loyalty, devotion,

Are these qualities an integral part of your relationship with the Lord?

Draw near to the Lord and ask Him to draw near to you.

▩ To meditate on

God wants to see His character in us. 'Those God foreknew he also predestined to be conformed to the likeness of his Son, that he might be the firstborn among many brothers' (Rom. 8:29).
'My dear children, for whom I am again in the pains of childbirth until Christ is formed in you' (Gal. 4:19).
'Be imitators of God, therefore, as dearly loved children' (Eph. 5:1).

"and make me wholly devoted to you"

divine promise behind it. So Jesus says, 'Remain in me' and then continues, 'and I will remain in you.' If we reach out to Him, He will release His power through us.

There are two ways in which the Lord remains in His people. He enters by His Spirit when we are 'born again'. Then He continues to abide in us beyond that point. The 'remaining' of John 15 does not concern the initial experience of new birth. It concerns the subsequent ministry of the Spirit as He works on our minds, emotions and wills and conforms us to the image of God's Son. Only when His righteousness, peace and joy flow out of our lives can we affect the lives of others.

If you want to be Jesus' disciple, you must understand His job description: the tension between your responsibility — to remain in Him, and His activity — to remain in you. If you don't grasp this, you are likely to slip into passivity and expect Jesus to do everything for you. But He says, 'Remain in Me — that's your job. My job is to release my activity in you. Unless I see you playing your part, I can't play mine. Your fruitfulness is dependent on your intimacy with Me.'

▩ Food for thought

➢ Read through the list of the fruit of the Spirit (Gal. 5:22,23).

➢ Spend time meditating on each fruit. Draw up a personal check-list to identify the fruit which is evident/missing in your life. (If you find self-assessment difficult, ask a friend whom you trust to help you.)

➢ Ask the Holy Spirit to work each fruit into your life and to make you grow and bear fruit in the lives of others.

▩ To discover

Name 3 characters in the Scriptures who were unfruitful.

____

____

____

What was the reason for their unfruitfulness?

____

____

... when the believer relies completely and continuously upon his Saviour and is obedient to His commands, then the life of Jesus inevitably flows into his life, so that he can truly say with Paul 'I live; yet not I, but Christ liveth in me' (Gal. 2:20).
R. V. G. Tasker

❑ STUDY 2

There before me was a throne in heaven with someone sitting on it. And the one who sat there had the appearance of jasper and carnelian. A rainbow, resembling an emerald, encircled the throne. Surrounding the throne were twenty-four other thrones, and seated on them were twenty-four elders ... From the throne came flashes of lightning, rumblings and peals of thunder. Before the throne, seven lamps were blazing. These are the seven spirits of God. Also before the throne there was what looked like a sea of glass, clear as crystal. In the centre, around the throne, were four living creatures ... they never stop saying: 'Holy, holy, holy is the Lord God Almighty, who was, and is, and is to come' (Rev. 4:2–8).

Fix your eyes on him

Revelation 4 helps us see the awesomeness of God. The chapter paints only a dim picture of the glorious throne, but it always thrills me and has often enriched my personal devotions. When I come to God, I often try to imagine this scene in heaven. You may find it an inspiration to you too.

The apostle John speaks of God as a real Person and struggles to find words to describe His glory. 'He's like jasper and carnelian,' he says. As far as I understand, these are green and red gems whose colours evidently merge and radiate from the Lord. A multicoloured rainbow encircles the throne, its seven colours somehow embraced by an emerald green.

Daniel tells us that there is a river of fire flowing from the throne (7:10). This is interesting because when Jesus returns with His holy angels, He will be revealed in blazing fire (2 Thess. 1:7). I picture the elders' thrones on either side of the river which I see flowing into the crystal sea. I try to imagine the flashes of lightning, rumblings and peals of thunder. And I visualise the seven spirits of God as they shine, and the four living creatures as they move around the throne and worship the Lord.

▩ To resolve

Resolve right now to spend some quality uninterrupted time with the Lord.

When will this be? ____________________

For how long? ________________________

Make a note to check up on yourself in a week's/fortnight's time to ensure that you have done this.

▩ To meditate on

Covet God's presence.
'If your Presence does not go with us, do not send us up from here' (Exod. 33:15).
'You will fill me with joy in your presence' (Ps. 16:11).
'In my integrity you uphold me and set me in your presence for ever' (Ps. 41:12).
'Do not cast me from your presence or take your Holy Spirit from me' (Ps. 51:11).

Paul declares that when we behold God's glory we are transformed into His likeness (2 Cor. 3:18). That's effectively what Jesus meant when He promised, 'I will remain in you.' We contemplate His glory, He responds by changing us and we reflect more of His glory.

All Christians have a general awareness of the Lord's presence. They may occasionally pray in tongues under their breath and hold an intermittent dialogue through the day. That's great. But it's not the same as spending uninterrupted time with God. David said, 'I was always beholding the LORD in my presence' (Acts 2:25a NASB). He set his mind on the Lord — and that's something we must do too.

God longs to meet with His children. Come to Him with earnest attentiveness and focused concentration. These are mental activities which aren't automatic, but unless you learn how to engage in them, your thoughts will travel around the world. You must do whatever is necessary to block all distractions. As you take time opening your spirit to God, pray that He will touch you. Express your love to Him. Bask in His presence. It's a truly wonderful experience.

Food for thought

➢ Read the following verses which mention God's presence. Psalm 16:7–11; 21:6,7; 31:19,20; 41:10–12; 51:7–12; 89:14–18; 90:7–10; 114; 139:7–10.

➢ What benefits are there in the Lord's presence? What is the Psalmist's attitude to the Lord's presence? What is your response to this?

To describe

Write down in a notebook your own description of Jesus' character and qualities, etc. in as many words as you can, then fill out the picture even more by reading through Revelation 4.

Use these notes to help you as you focus on Jesus when you come into His presence.

... we must not lose sight of the fact that knowing God is an emotional relationship, as well as an intellectual and volitional one, and could not indeed be a deep relation between persons were it not so.
J. I. Packer

❑ STUDY 3

Waiting on God

Mary ... sat at the Lord's feet listening to what he said. But Martha was distracted by all the preparations that had to be made. She came to him and asked, 'Lord, don't you care that my sister has left me to do the work by myself? Tell her to help me!' 'Martha, Martha,' the Lord answered, 'you are worried and upset about many things, but only one thing is needed. Mary has chosen what is better, and it will not be taken away from her' (Luke 10:39–42).

There's a saying: 'What you can live without, you will do without.' It's true with regard to the Kingdom of God. If you decide, 'I can live without signs and wonders,' God won't give them to you. And if you say, 'I can manage without intimate contact with Jesus,' then He won't force Himself on you.

How often the following kind of dialogue must be repeated today!

Christian: Lord, I can't live without You.
God: Right, then you must wait on Me.
Christian: But I don't really want to do that.
God: Well, you can live without Me.
Christian: No, I can't! I need Your presence.
God: If you can't live without it, you won't be without it! You are only as close to Me as you want to be. I will give to you according to your hunger.

Often our problem is that life is simply too distracting. We look around us and see so many alluring things — the sun, the beach, the sea, the countryside, the TV. We want to be having fun with our family or friends, enjoying God's world, drinking in its pleasures. There's nothing essentially wrong with these things, but there's a tug on our lives. We aren't

▩ To consider

When you wait on the Lord, what are your distractions?

People + their needs; ______

______

What practical steps can you take towards greater concentration?

______

______

▩ To meditate on

The Christian life involves effort.
'Make every effort to add to your faith goodness; and to goodness, knowledge; and to knowledge, self-control; and to self-control, perseverance; and to perseverance, godliness; and to godliness, brotherly kindness; and to brotherly kindness, love' (2 Pet. 1:5–7).
'Make every effort to be found spotless, blameless and at peace with him' (2 Pet. 3:14).

"Work out your own salvation with fear and trembling" Phil 2 v 12.

children of this evil age; we're children of the resurrection. The world isn't worthy of us and it will never bring us complete satisfaction.

Waiting on God involves a conscious deliberate activity requiring commitment, time and energy. We must 'make every effort to enter [God's] rest' (Heb. 4:11a). The 'effort' is against our flesh which wants to do anything but sit and wait for God. The 'rest' is not inactivity, but a calm confidence that God will respond. So my carnal mind might be in a hundred places, screaming 'No!' to spiritual pursuits and I will be saying, 'I'm going to fight, Lord. I believe that you will intervene if I persist in this.'

The amount of effort will depend very much on the degree to which we are familiar with the presence of God. The more unaccustomed we are to waiting on Him, the more of a struggle it will be to spend time with Him. When we come to Him, we will feel uncomfortable. Our minds will be full of our own thoughts and it will be hard to open ourselves up and hear His voice. After a month or so of struggling we may be tempted to think, 'This is hopeless. I'm giving up.' Let me encourage you to keep at it — because it's worth it.

▩ Food for thought

- ➢ Read Luke 11:5–8; 18:1–8.
- ➢ What do these two parables teach us about persistence in prayer?
- ➢ How long do we need to persist?
- ➢ How does this affect your perspective on 'unanswered prayer'?
- ➢ Is there anything which you need to persist in prayer for?

▩ To pray

How close to the Lord do you want to be?

If you have a 'take it or leave it' attitude towards the Lord you will never become intimate with Him.

Tell the Lord how much you need Him, ask for His help in disciplining yourself to wait on Him.

That is why meditation is so threatening to us. It boldly calls us to enter into the living presence of God for ourselves. It tells us that God is speaking in the continuous present and wants to address us. Jesus and the New Testament writers make clear that this is not just for the religious professionals — the priests — but for everyone.
Richard Foster

❑ STUDY 4

Consistency then anointing

'When you give a banquet, invite the poor, the crippled, the lame, the blind, and you will be blessed' (Luke 14:13,14a).

'Give, and it will be given to you. A good measure, pressed down, shaken together and running over, will be poured into your lap. For with the measure you use, it will be measured to you' (Luke 6:38).

'Jesus told his disciples ... that they should always pray and not give up' (Luke 18:1).

'The time will come when the bridegroom will be taken from them; in those days they will fast' (Luke 5:35).

One of the principles of the Kingdom of God is this: that the Lord calls for consistency in routine before He gives us His anointing. This offends some people. 'I'm happy to spend time in prayer,' they say, 'but only if I know that God is going to anoint me on the spot.' God replies, 'No. You spend time beholding me and I will release my activity in you when I decide.'

Smith Wigglesworth, who was mightily used in healing, said of spiritual disciplines, 'I start in the flesh and end in the Spirit.' Now there are certain Kingdom activities that you daren't start in the flesh because you won't end up in the Spirit. But this is not true of the devotional disciplines. What Wigglesworth meant was that he would begin without any great leading from the Lord and experience God's inspiration later.

In Matthew 6:1–18, Jesus describes four disciplines that we should do secretly, without inspiration, knowing that He will reward us afterwards. The first of these concerns 'acts of righteousness' — our loving actions towards others. Serving people involves inconvenience but it reveals our devotion to the Lord.

The second discipline is 'giving to the needy' — faithfulness in the area of finance. I believe

▩ To pray

Pray that Christians will begin to see the importance of spiritual discipline and begin to seek God more whole-heartedly than ever before.

▩ To meditate on

God wants us to know Him.
'Be still, and know that I am God' (Ps. 46:10a).
'This is eternal life: that they may know you, the only true God, and Jesus Christ, whom you have sent' (John 17:3).
'I consider everything a loss compared to the surpassing greatness of knowing Christ Jesus my Lord' (Phil. 3:8a).

that the tithe needs to go to the local church, and offerings to others as the Lord directs.

The third discipline is 'prayer'. Paul exhorts us to 'Devote [ourselves] to prayer' (Col. 4:2).

The fourth discipline is 'fasting'. If you're not already fasting, I would encourage you to ask God to commission you to engage in this. I know many believers who fast once a week because they realise that fasting is a vital part of New Testament Christianity.

So we start off with discipline. We're tired and feeling totally unspiritual but we sit or kneel down, open our Bible and begin to read and pray. Sometimes the sort of anointing that we want doesn't come. But that's essentially not our problem. Our business is to behold the Lord and His business is to transform us. The promise stands that if we engage in secret spiritual disciplines, God will reward us openly — in His way and time.

God wants us to be concerned about our secret history with Him. It's nothing to do with legalistic striving. It's to do with relationship — getting to know Him better. He's calling us away from the busyness of life into a deeper communion with Him. Let's rise to that.

Food for thought

➢ Prayerfully consider each of the four disciplines mentioned in this study.

➢ What is God saying to you in regard to:

- your service?
- your giving?
- your prayer life?
- your fasting?

➢ Set yourself realistic goals in each area, e.g. I will miss one meal a week/fortnight and spend the time praying.

To discover

Read through Matthew 6:1–18 and discover what Jesus has to say about the four disciplines mentioned in the text.

Memorise any of the verses which are particularly relevant to you.

The emphasis of our age is on serving God, accomplishing things for God. Enoch was a preacher of righteousness in a day of gross ungodliness, but God saw fit that the brief account of his life emphasized that he walked with God. What are we training ourselves for? Are we training ourselves only in Christian activity, as good as that may be, or are we training ourselves first of all in godliness?
Jerry Bridges

❑ STUDY 5

Do not be deceived, God is not mocked; for whatever a man sows, this he will also reap. For the one who sows to his own flesh shall from the flesh reap corruption, but the one who sows to the Spirit shall from the Spirit reap eternal life. And let us not lose heart in doing good, for in due time we shall reap if we do not grow weary (Gal. 6:7–9 NASB).

You reap what you sow

When Paul warns us, 'Do not be deceived', we must take note because he's speaking with good reason. One of the ways we can be deceived is to think that we won't reap what we sow. While we know that a farmer doesn't plant a crop one day and see it mature the next, we can forget that this same 'time delay' between sowing and reaping applies to everyone.

The wicked are deceived. They happily 'sow to the flesh' without a second thought. They satisfy their lustful desires and walk away thinking, 'I don't feel any different.' Then they repeat their actions and conclude, 'I'm no great pervert. This isn't hurting me.' They assume that they're all right because nothing adverse happens to them. The truth is that they are storing up wrath against themselves and sooner or later God's judgement will come.

Sadly, believers can fall into the same deception. I remember talking to a guy who told me that there was so much immorality in his mind that he couldn't sit in the prayer meeting without being hounded by evil thoughts. The fact was that for many months he had faithfully given himself to pornography. Initially, he had probably thought, 'This is nothing serious.

▩ To confess

Are you mocking God in any way, e.g. is there some secret sin?

Confess to the Lord any lack of obedience in your life and resolve to act on His Word.

▩ To meditate on

God is not mocked.
'God "will give to each person according to what he has done". To those who by persistence in doing good seek glory, honour and immortality, he will give eternal life. But for those who are self-seeking and who reject the truth and follow evil, there will be wrath and anger' (Rom. 2:6–8).
'(God) rewards those who earnestly seek him' (Heb. 11:6b).

Maybe God doesn't notice.' But God was not mocked. This man was now bound by lustful thoughts. He was reaping what he had sown.

Many Christians give up on spiritual disciplines because they don't see God's immediate intervention. I often used to quit praying to God. I recall telling Him, 'Lord, I really do love you. It's just that I don't like talking to you. Perhaps it's because you don't reply very loudly!' I simply didn't believe that discipline was relevant. I didn't see that it related to an increase in righteousness and I doubted that God was doing anything.

But the great Judge doesn't tell us to remain in Him, to behold Him and to sow to the Spirit without responding in an appropriate way. He is not mocked. If you give yourself fully to acts of righteousness, generosity, prayer and fasting He will reward you — it's a promise.

You may think that your sowing isn't very effective. Day by day you may be serving and crying out to Him — but with little apparent response. Will you be deceived? Or will you declare to Him, 'Lord, you say that if I sow to the Spirit, you will release your life in me; I believe you and I'm going to persevere'?

▩ Food for thought

➢ Read Psalms 1:4–6; 10:13–15; 37:12–15; 73; Proverbs 5:21–23; Ecclesiastes 8:11–13; Acts 5:1–10. Write down in a notebook the way that God responds to the wicked.

➢ Pray specifically for groups of people who are bent on evil, e.g. drug pushers, rapists, liars, deceivers, etc. Ask God to have mercy on them and save them.

➢ Pray for the effectiveness of the police force — particularly in reference to any local or national incident that has happened recently, e.g. a murder or rape.

▩ To consider

Note down the curses that Adam and Eve reaped for us when they sowed to the flesh (Gen. 3:16–24).

____

____

Note down some of the blessings that Christ reaped for us when He sowed to the Spirit.

____

____

I defy you to read the life of any saint that has ever adorned the life of the Church without seeing at once that the greatest characteristic in the life of that saint was discipline and order.
Martyn Lloyd-Jones

❑ STUDY 6

A God who hides Himself

'If only I knew where to find him; if only I could go to his dwelling! ... But if I go to the east, he is not there; if I go to the west, I do not find him. When he is at work in the north, I do not see him; when he turns to the south, I catch no glimpse of him. But he knows the way that I take; when he has tested me, I shall come forth as gold. My feet have closely followed his steps; I have kept to his way without turning aside. I have not departed from the commands of his lips; I have treasured the words of his mouth more than my daily bread' (Job 23:3,8–12).

God rarely works in accordance with our expectations. There we are, serving wholeheartedly, praying fervently, fasting regularly — and there's absolutely no sign of God's powerful intervention. We protest, 'Lord, I've been seeking you earnestly and nothing's happening. I'm fulfilling my part of the bargain, but where are you? I'm offended. It isn't fair.'

If God is silent for long enough, we can assume that He hasn't noticed us. We see Him as a kind of chef who's flying around the kitchen. His attention is always on someone else while we sit indefinitely on the back burner screaming, 'Lord, I'm about to boil over and burn dry. Don't you realise?' Then we imagine His turning to us with a startled look and saying, 'Gee, I'm sorry. I'd completely forgotten you. Have you been crying out to me for long?'

I've pondered this problem a lot. From our point of view it would make logical sense for God always to provide instant answers — because then people would pray much more! But His ways and thoughts are higher than ours. When He makes us wait, it's not because He's forgotten us but because He is working out a greater plan than we can as yet see. He's

▩ To memorise

Memorise Isaiah 40:27,28.

The complaint is, 'Why doesn't God see what's happening?'

Why do you think that the reply is, 'Look at God'?

____

____

▩ To meditate on

Sometimes God hides Himself from us. 'God left (Hezekiah) to test him and to know everything that was in his heart' (2 Chr. 32:31b).
'I cry to you for help, O LORD; in the morning my prayer comes before you. Why, O LORD, do you reject me and hide your face from me?' (Ps. 88:13,14).
'Truly you are a God who hides himself' (Isa. 45:15a).

our heavenly Father. He's infinitely wiser than we are. And He knows exactly what He's doing.

So we can be thoroughly faithful, and He can remain totally silent. That's His prerogative. He is Lord. Indeed, we should expect God to withdraw from us periodically — it's a Kingdom principle. The Scriptures and great heroes of faith all testify to the God who hides Himself.

Your reaction to God's seasons of silence will determine the quality of your faith. If you are offended, you are likely to slip into self-pity and complaint. You will be irritated, annoyed and resistant to what God is doing in your life. And you will probably give up on the spiritual disciplines because 'they don't work'.

But if you are wise, you will recognise that there's purpose in silence. You may not like it, but by faith you will accept it and rejoice that God is aware of what He's doing. You will also remain diligent in the spiritual disciplines, knowing that God will see your consistency and respond with His release and anointing.

While you wait on God, He will work humility and gratitude into you and prepare you for the future. Don't take this challenge lightly. In due time you will reap — if you don't give up.

▩ Food for thought

➢ Look at what God had to say to Job when He questioned him (Job 38—42:6).

➢ Write down in a notebook what you understand:

- about God.
- about yourself.

▩ To ask

When you have experienced 'seasons of silence' in the past, what has your response been?

____

____

Make a list in a notebook of Scriptures which will encourage you at such a time, e.g. 'I will never leave you nor forsake you' (Josh. 1:5b).

If the Spirit can teach us ... that there is no danger in leaving with Him the time and the means of answering our prayer, our seasons of prayer will become in truth seasons of rest. We shall begin to see that it is God's will not only to hear our prayer, but to give us the best and the richest answer which He, the almighty and omniscient God, can devise.
O. Hallesby

❑ STUDY 7

You did not receive a spirit that makes you a slave again to fear, but you received the Spirit of sonship. And by him we cry, '*Abba*, Father.' The Spirit himself testifies with our spirit that we are God's children (Rom. 8:15,16).

They that wait upon the LORD shall renew *their* strength; they shall mount up with wings as eagles; they shall run, and not be weary; *and* they shall walk, and not faint (Isa. 40:31 AV).

The 'Abba' cry

The cry, 'Abba, Father' is not simply a call for God's attention, it's an exclamation of intimate recognition. The Spirit in us says, 'You belong to God,' and we reply, 'Yes, I know. Abba, Daddy! It's true! I'm yours!'

A holy addiction grips people who wait in the presence of God. In the same way as the rich are compelled to get richer, so those who pray are gripped by an increasing desire to pray. The longer you're with God, the more the Holy Spirit stirs you to cry out for Him and the more time you want to spend in His presence.

Usually I encourage people to pray for half an hour every day. The apparent brevity of this period of time doesn't concern me because I've never seen true disciples continue to spend only thirty minutes a day in God's company. If they're consistent and obedient, He will pursue them. After a while, they won't be satisfied with 30 minutes, they'll go on for 45, then an hour and finally they'll be sneaking off to be with God as often as they can.

I've seen it happen. Christians who were almost indifferent about prayer suddenly began touching the throne of God and finding that they couldn't drag themselves away. After a

▩ To review

Make a list of all your activities in any given week.

What do you spend most time on?

____

What changes do you feel you should make?

____

▩ To meditate on

God satisfies our hunger.
'The lions may grow weak and hungry, but those who seek the LORD lack no good thing' (Ps. 34:10).
'He satisfies the thirsty and fills the hungry with good things' (Ps. 107:9).
'Blessed are you who hunger now, for you will be satisfied' (Luke 6:21a).
'He who comes to me will never go hungry, and he who believes in me will never be thirsty' (John 6:35b).

year or two their televisions were almost redundant and former priorities were turned on their heads. Certainly, they continued to be responsible at work and made time for their families. It's just that as they prayed, the Spirit enlarged their capacity for God and they had to satisfy their desire for Him.

We can't create a hunger for God; it's supernaturally imparted to us by the Spirit. It doesn't come to us if we have a certain kind of temperament; it's given to us if we wait on God. He doesn't force us to spend time with Him. Rather, He leaves us with the choice.

Many of us long for a deeper passion for God. We know that Jesus was consumed with zeal for His Father's house (John 2:17) but we feel hopelessly unzealous. The fact is that we can't change our emotions, but we can change our minds. We can decide to wait on God — and those who do that will renew their strength.

Wherever you lack strength, ask God for help. Cry out, 'Lord, give me zeal! I want a new hunger for you.' Keep praying; keep waiting on Him; keep giving yourself to His Word. God will fan the flames, change your feelings and transform your relationship with Him.

▩ Food for thought

➢ In a notebook draw a line down the centre of a page. In the left-hand column write down all the good qualities *and* all the failings of your earthly father.

➢ In the right-hand column write down the corresponding perfect qualities of your heavenly Father.

➢ Spend time meditating on your child/Father relationship with God. Thank Him for His wonderful love towards you.

▩ To ask

What do you need from God, e.g. zeal, compassion, strength, faith, etc.?

____

____

Spend time crying out to God for this.

'Our Father which art in heaven!' **To appreciate this word of adoration aright, I must remember that none of the saints had in Scripture ever ventured to address God as their Father. The invocation places us at once in the centre of the wonderful revelation the Son came to make of His Father as our Father too.**
Andrew Murray
With Christ in the School of Prayer

❑ STUDY 8

To behold and to inquire

Do not be anxious about anything, but in everything, by prayer and petition, with thanksgiving, present your requests to God (Phil. 4:6).

Come, let us bow down in worship, let us kneel before the LORD our Maker (Ps. 95:6).

Oh, how I love your law! I meditate on it all day long (Ps. 119:97).

I thank God that I speak in tongues more than all of you (1 Cor. 14:18).

'The LORD is in his holy temple; let all the earth be silent before him' (Hab. 2:20).

God wants us to come to Him and change. Let's look at five of the ways in which we can behold Him.

Prayer. Catch the wonder of this: you can open your spirit to God, sense His presence and pray His blessing on someone right over the other side of the world! If you quietly vocalise your prayers, you will find it easier to concentrate because your mind will follow your voice. Even if you don't see immediate results, believe that your prayers are having an impact in heaven.

Worship. Praise needs an object. It's no use singing songs while your mind is all over the place and then thinking, 'I worshipped God today.' You have to focus your full attention on Jesus and actually declare to Him how you feel. God is looking for worshippers who worship in Spirit and truth. Let's be fervent both in private and when we're praising God together.

Meditation. Jesus said, 'You diligently study the Scriptures because you think that by them you possess eternal life, yet you refuse to come to me to have life' (John 5:39,40). At one time I was studying the Bible really hard but couldn't understand why I felt so far from God. Then I realised that although I was seeking knowledge,

▩ To discover

How does the Bible encourage us to worship God? List in a notebook as many ways as you can find, e.g. singing, kneeling, etc.

Does your worship incorporate all of these?

What might God be saying to you about this?

▩ To meditate on

We are called into fellowship with God. 'One thing have I desired of the LORD, that will I seek after; that I may dwell in the house of the LORD all the days of my life, to behold the beauty of the LORD, and to inquire in his temple' (Ps. 27:4 AV).

'Father, I desire that they also, whom Thou hast given Me, be with Me where I am, in order that they may behold My glory, which Thou hast given Me' (John 17:24a NASB).

I wasn't coming to Jesus for life. Sometimes the difference between study and meditation is this: study simply informs the mind while meditation enhances the heart. Meditation turns a Scripture into a conversation with Jesus and 'washes' us (Eph. 5:26). It's good to study; it's better to meditate — because meditation exposes our spirit to Jesus in a direct way.

Tongues. An evangelical Christian once said to me, 'The trouble with charismatics is that all they do is speak in tongues.' I became the pastor of a charismatic group and I concluded, 'The trouble with charismatics is that they rarely speak in tongues.' Some of us pray in tongues a couple of times a week and decide that, 'It doesn't do much for me.' But there are some experiences of the Spirit that come only after you've prayed in tongues for an hour or more. Let me challenge you periodically to pray in the Spirit for a couple of hours and see what happens. You might need to continue this practice for a year, but it will change your life.

Silence. Sometimes you will come to God and the Spirit will groan inside you. On other occasions you will feel overwhelmed by His presence and be content to sit and enjoy Him.

▩ Food for thought

➢ Spend time making a comprehensive list in a notebook of *all* that you can give thanks for — large and small, ordinary and extraordinary.

➢ The Psalmist encourages us to 'Enter his gates with thanksgiving and his courts with praise; give thanks to him and praise his name' (Ps. 100:4).

➢ Use the list you have made as an aide-memoire whenever you come into the Lord's presence.

▩ To plan

Set yourself realistic goals in each of these areas, e.g. I will pray in tongues for 10 minutes each morning.

Prayer____________________

Worship ____________________

Meditation____________________

Tongues____________________

Silence ____________________

We are to be shut out from men, and shut in with God.
Andrew Murray

❑ STUDY 9

No other foundation can any one lay than that which is laid, which is Jesus Christ. Now if any one builds on the foundation with gold, silver, precious stones, wood, hay, stubble — each man's work will become manifest; for the Day will disclose it, because it will be revealed with fire, and the fire will test what sort of work each one has done. If the work which any man has built on the foundation survives, he will receive a reward. If any man's work is burned up, he will suffer loss, though he himself will be saved, but only as through fire (1 Cor. 3:11b–15 RSV).

As through fire

In 1974 and 1978 God gave me two similar supernatural visions. I'd like to share the later one with you.

I was kneeling before the judgement seat of Christ and gazing up at the Lord. I couldn't see His face in a human way, but by the Spirit I understood His reactions. He looked at me and said, 'Saved, as through fire.' Then He added, 'Saved, but your life was wasted.'

Horror gripped me. I tried to persuade Him to change His evaluation of me. In a split second, I brought all my arguments to Him, but it was clear from His stern face that He would not be manipulated. So I began pleading with Him for a second chance, but He wouldn't respond to that either. I was in anguish. It was the last day; God wouldn't change His mind; there was no second chance and I'd totally failed to bear the fruit that He'd ordained for me. When the vision faded, I was on the floor, sobbing and crying out to Him with all my heart.

It wasn't an issue of salvation, but of fruitfulness. God was putting before me two paths and showing me what would happen if I took the wrong one — the common one, the one that most Christians take.

▩ To imagine

Imagine that it is the last day and *you* are before the judgement seat. What would be Jesus' verdict on you?

____

____

What can you do now to improve that verdict?

____

▩ To meditate on

We should not be ashamed of Jesus. 'If anyone is ashamed of me and my words, the Son of Man will be ashamed of him when he comes' (Luke 9:26a). 'He who is coming will come and will not delay. But my righteous one will live by faith. And if he shrinks back, I will not be pleased with him' (Heb. 10:37b,38). 'And now, dear children, continue in him, so that when he appears we may be confident and unashamed before him at his coming' (1 John 2:28).

Many believers don't like thinking about judgement day. But ignoring it doesn't change the fact that it will come. Sooner or later we will all stand before the throne, gaze into Jesus' eyes and give account of ourselves to Him. What will be important then? Not what I think about my life, but what He thinks. Will He reward my work because I did it solely for His glory, or burn it because I did it for mine?

Both visions had a profound effect on me, and so did something God said to me in 1976 — which was, 'I don't want you just to echo everything you hear. I want you to know my voice in your heart and to speak under the unction of the Spirit.' Suddenly, I didn't want to have second-hand information and a powerless ministry. I didn't want to go the common way. I didn't want to hear God say to me on the last day, 'I gave you my Son, the Holy Spirit, the Word and my divine calling — and what did you do? You served yourself like all the others.'

Even now I can feel the desperation I felt during the visions. And even now I respond with all my heart, 'No, God! I'm not going to waste my life. I'm going to be 100 per cent committed to the things that are relevant to you.'

▩ Food for thought

➢ Read Ezekiel 1:25–28; Daniel 10:4–10; Revelation 1:10–17.

➢ Write down in a notebook how Jesus appeared to these three prophets. What was their response?

➢ Spend time worshipping the Lord, focusing especially on His glory.

▩ To examine

Look up Romans 14:10; 2 Corinthians 5:10; Hebrews 4:13.

Examine your response to these verses.

Is it one of fear or confident assurance?

Ask the Lord to help you produce fruit that will remain.

At the Day of Judgement, we shall not be asked what we have read, but what we have done; not how eloquently we have spoken, but how holily we have lived.
Thomas à Kempis

❑ STUDY 10

The one God esteems

(Jesus said) '"You cannot serve both God and Money." The Pharisees, who loved money, heard all this and were sneering at Jesus. He said to them, "You are the ones who justify yourselves in the eyes of men, but God knows your hearts. What is highly valued among men is detestable in God's sight"' (Luke 16:13b–15).

'Because you are lukewarm — neither hot nor cold — I am about to spit you out of my mouth' (Rev. 3:16).

'This is the one I esteem: he who is humble and contrite in spirit, and trembles at my word' (Isa. 66:2b).

People throughout the ages applaud things that are irrelevant to God. The religious leaders of Jesus' day loved money, but sneered at Jesus when He told them, 'It's either God or mammon.' His priorities found no place in their hearts and they hated Him.

One of the great needs of the church today is to be able to esteem what God esteems and to despise what He despises. Many Christians fail to do this. They see an influential leader and idolise him, but they don't detect the carnality behind his messages. What they parade as wonderful, God spits out of His mouth.

The early church had trouble with worldly individuals. Jude wrote, 'Certain men ... have secretly slipped in among you. They are godless men, who change the grace of our God into a licence for immorality' (Jude v.4a). God's grace should teach us 'to say "No" to ungodliness and worldly passions' (Titus 2:12b). But there are many who preach grace in such a way that it gives us security while we continue to sin. The world praises them; God is repulsed.

Sometimes believers simply rely on their church leaders or others to be their chief guides in life. So when you want to know if

▩ To discover

Look up the word *contrite* in a dictionary. What does it mean?

____

____

What is a contrite Christian?

____

Are you contrite?

▩ To meditate on

We must live by the Word of God. 'Blessed are they whose ways are blameless, who walk according to the law of the Lord ... I have set my heart on your laws ... I will always obey your law, for ever and ever ... I will hasten and not delay to obey your commands ... Oh, how I love your law! Direct my footsteps according to your word; let no sin rule over me ... give me understanding according to your word' (Ps. 119:1,30b,44,60,97a,133,169b).

you're doing OK, you just ask them, they give you their opinion and you just take their word for it. You don't have to work out your own salvation any more. Others can do it for you!

It's also becoming fashionable to compare yourself with others. 'I've got much higher standards than Jo,' we think. But the apostle Paul never dared to compare himself with anyone else and said that those who did were 'not wise'. He knew that the only praise worth having was from the Lord.

On the last day we will all stand before Someone who will not evaluate us by what others say, but by His eternal Word (John 12:48). This being the case, how well do we measure up to the standards in the Bible? Do our hearts tremble at the thought that one day we will be judged by it?

Many Christians must re-evaluate their lives. They've been following the advice of others and failing to see that God despises what they're doing. The Bible is our touchstone. If our opinions aren't consistent with it, we don't rationalise them, we throw them out. Do you want God to esteem you? Then be humble and contrite in spirit, and tremble at His Word.

▩ Food for thought

➢ Study 2 Corinthians 10:12–18 and Jeremiah 9:23–24.

➢ In the light of these Scriptures make an assessment of yourself.

➢ What adjustments do you need to make?

➢ Ask the Lord to help you see yourself as He sees you and for His transforming grace to be at work in your life.

▩ To ascertain

Write down three things that God esteems but man doesn't, e.g. love for enemies.

____

____

____

What are you doing that God esteems and man doesn't?

____

The whole purpose of our salvation is that we be "holy and blameless in His sight" (Ephesians 1:4). To continue to live in sin as a Christian is to go contrary to God's very purpose for our salvation.
Jerry Bridges

❑ **STUDY 11**

Living for His glory

'The axe is already at the root of the trees, and every tree that does not produce good fruit will be cut down and thrown into the fire' (Matt. 3:10).

If anyone's name was not found written in the book of life, he was thrown into the lake of fire (Rev. 20:15).

Since, then, you have been raised with Christ, set your hearts on things above, where Christ is seated at the right hand of God. Set your minds on things above, not on earthly things. For you died, and your life is now hidden with Christ in God. When Christ, who is your life, appears, then you also will appear with him in glory (Col. 3:1–4).

God wants to impress on us the reality of the judgement to come. John the Baptist preached this theme when he appeared in the wilderness, and judgement was an integral part of Paul's message too (Acts 24:25a). It's a terrifying subject for the unbeliever who, if he fails to repent, will be thrown into the lake of fire and left there, in torment, for ever.

On the last day, God's judgement fire will fall not on the believer, but on his work which will be 'shown for what it is' (1 Cor. 3:13a). Any actions that have not been initiated by God will burn up in an instant, and people who have sought mainly to build a name for themselves will be humbled.

A fresh vision of judgement forces us to realise how pointless it is to establish our little ministries which are motivated by self-interest and pride. Suddenly we see that God will honour only what He has originated and begin crying out to Him, 'Lord, don't shock me then, shock me now! Show me the truth about myself in an age when I can change.'

Our roots are in another Kingdom. We are living for eternity. Our portion is Jesus, not increase in ministry or public acclaim. God has

▩ To repent

Read Psalm 139:23,24.

Is the Father behind every ministry or activity that you are involved in?

Repent of any selfish motivation and pray that the Lord will lead you into any ministry He has for you.

▩ To meditate on

Jesus lived only for His Father.
'I have come down from heaven not to do my will but to do the will of him who sent me' (John 6:38).
'The Son can do nothing by himself; he can do only what he sees his Father doing, because whatever the Father does the Son also does' (John 5:19b).
'I always do what pleases him' (John 8:29b).
'If I glorify myself, my glory means nothing' (John 8:54a).

called us to glorify His Son, not ourselves, and in the brief moment that we have on earth, it's not worth being driven by selfish desires and ambitions.

While worldly thinking tempts us to seek the applause of men, God's Word tells us to adopt the attitude of Christ (Phil. 2:5–11). Jesus never pushed Himself forward. He never sought popularity or promoted His own ministry. Rather the opposite. When people tried to make Him King, He didn't get all excited and think, 'Wow! They believe I'm Someone special. What a terrific opportunity to prove them right!' Why not? Because He could do only what His Father told Him. God said, 'No', so Jesus withdrew to a mountain by Himself (John 6:15).

If you have one eye on the judgement seat, you will be very careful how you live. You will neither manipulate situations to your best advantage, nor allow others to force you prematurely into a place of prominence that God hasn't given to you. Rather, you'll think, 'The Father isn't behind this so it's folly to accept it. If He has a significant ministry for me, He'll give it to me in His time. I can do only what He says.'

Food for thought

➢ Meditate on Revelation 20:11–15.

➢ Pray that God will give you:

- a deeper awareness of the fate of sinners.
- an increased longing to see their salvation.
- a greater willingness to share Jesus with them.

➢ Pray more earnestly for 'divine appointments' and take them up whenever they come.

To understand

Read Genesis 11:1–8.

What did the people want to do?

___

What happened?

___

What understanding does this give you?

___

... if we would know God, it is vital that we face the truth concerning His wrath, however unfashionable it may be, and however strong our initial prejudices against it.
J. I. Packer

❑ STUDY 12

A heart of wisdom

Moses:
Teach us to number our days aright, that we may gain a heart of wisdom (Ps. 90:12).

David:
'Show me, O LORD, my life's end and the number of my days; let me know how fleeting is my life. You have made my days a mere handbreadth; the span of my years is as nothing before you. Each man's life is but a breath. Man is a mere phantom as he goes to and fro: He bustles about, but only in vain; he heaps up wealth, not knowing who will get it' (Ps. 39:4–6).

God wants us to see our lives in the light of eternity. Like Moses and David, we need to understand how short our sojourn on earth really is, then we won't fritter away time doing things that He hasn't initiated. A 'heart of wisdom' is not found in those who are trying to prove to others that they can make it to the top, but in those who are interested solely in serving and pleasing the Lord.

Solomon says, 'A wise son brings joy to his father' (Prov. 10:1a). Jesus did that. He 'numbered His days' and wouldn't allow Himself to be side-tracked from God's purposes. We too are on earth for a brief moment. According to David, our days are a 'mere handbreadth' and to James, we are 'a mist that appears for a little while and then vanishes' (James 4:14b).

The apostle John tells us not to pursue 'the cravings of sinful man, the lust of his eyes and the boasting of what he has and does'. Why does he say this? Because he's wise enough to realise that 'the world and its desires pass away' (1 John 2:16b,17a). Sensuality, greed and pride don't exist in eternity. They belong to a fleeting age — but it will tempt us to waste our lives and lose our fruitfulness.

To pray

Pray through Psalm 39:4 with David. As you do so ask the Lord if you are being seduced by the world in any area of your life.

If so, put it right with the Lord now.

To meditate on

Life is transient and fragile.
'All men are like grass, and all their glory is like the flowers of the field. The grass withers and the flowers fall, because the breath of the LORD blows on them' (Isa. 40:6b,7a).
'The sun rises with scorching heat and withers the plant; its blossom falls and its beauty is destroyed. In the same way, the rich man will fade away even while he goes about his business' (James 1:11).

John continues, 'but the man who does the will of God lives for ever' (1 John 2:17b). We have been born for eternal life, that's why it's so foolish to give ourselves to temporal pleasures. Who would be stupid enough to invest in a bankrupt system, to give all his passion, time and energy to something that wasn't going to last?

A Christian once told me that he'd been cheated of $5,000. He was extremely bitter about it and I really wasn't very sympathetic. As far as I was concerned, he was a child of the Kingdom who had been seduced into wasting his life thinking about the injustice to which he'd been subjected.

We mustn't be so easily offended, so quick to make an uproar about nothing. Certainly you'll be annoyed if you're ripped off or overlooked, but you're only a 'mere phantom' and you can take nothing into eternity with you anyway. So there's no point in wasting time resenting something that someone else has done to you when you could be living for God. If He's pleased with you, that should be all that matters. You must gain a 'heart of wisdom' in this passing evil age.

▩ Food for thought

➢ Look up the following Scriptures: Prov. 1:7; 2:2,6,10,12; 8:11; 9:10; 16:16; 24:14; 28:26. or use a concordance to do a word study on *wisdom*.

➢ What is wisdom? How do we get wisdom? What are the benefits of wisdom?

▩ To beware

Are you harbouring bitterness or a grudge towards anyone about something in the past or present?

Has this made you lose sight of your goal?

What steps will you take to deal with this, e.g. reconciliation?

Wherever you are, Jesus Christ (the Rock) is ready to take over the foundation of your house. He'll personally remove all the sand and replace it with Himself. He'll take you just as you are — finite, troubled, argumentative, broken, fragmented, disillusioned, confused, and sinful. And He'll make you like you ought to be. Your years may be few, but they need not be futile.
Charles Swindoll

❑ STUDY 13

Be faithful to your calling

'It will be like a man going on a journey, who called his servants and entrusted his property to them. To one he gave five talents of money, to another two talents, and to another one talent, each according to his ability. Then he went on his journey. The man who had received the five talents went at once and put his money to work and gained five more. So also, the one with the two talents ... But the man who had received the one talent went off, dug a hole in the ground and hid his master's money. After a long time the master of those servants returned and settled accounts with them'
(Matt. 25:14–19).

Every Christian has two callings: in this age and in the one to come. We don't know anything about our individual role in eternity, but we can get involved in God's plans for us here on earth. Indeed, there's a continuity between now and the future. The seventy years or so that we have here is preparing us for everlasting life in heaven.

Several parables suggest that our yield will be according to the way we invest — not only now but also in the coming age. When we faithfully do what God has given us, He will bless our work in the present and will also give us further reward in heaven. If, on the other hand, we squander our time on this passing age, we will suffer loss both here and in eternity. That's why the apostle John warns us, 'Watch out that you do not lose what you have worked for, but that you may be rewarded fully' (2 John v.8).

John also urges us to 'continue in him, so that when he appears we may be confident and unashamed before him at his coming' (1 John 2:28). Although all believers will enter the eternal city, they will not all receive equal rewards. On the day of evaluation there will

▩ To consider

What earthly rewards does God give to those who are obedient? (Give Scriptures to back up your statements.)

____

____

____

____

▩ To meditate on

We must be ready for Jesus' return.
'May (the Lord) strengthen your hearts so that you will be blameless and holy in the presence of our God and Father when our Lord Jesus comes with all his holy ones' (1 Thess. 3:13).
'You ought to live holy and godly lives as you look forward to the day of God and speed its coming ... make every effort to be found spotless, blameless and at peace with him'
(2 Pet. 3:11b,12a,14b).

clearly be some who will be ashamed and others who will be confident. Those who hang their heads will be bitterly regretting the way that they have wasted their lives and given themselves to things that God has not ordained for them to do. Those whose heads are held high will be rejoicing that while they were on earth they put great value on their time and gave themselves whole-heartedly to God's calling on their lives.

When John exhorts us to 'continue in him', he calls to mind the words of Jesus, 'Remain in me' (John 15:4a). If you abide in Christ, you won't have to draw back in shame when He appears. That's because you will be waiting on Him, listening to Him and wrapped up in His purposes for your life.

I want to invest for the present and for eternity, but my greater interest lies in building for eternity. If Jesus gives me two talents, I want to be able to stand before Him on the day of judgement and say, 'Lord, here's your return. I haven't tried to be greater or less than you created me to be. I've been completely faithful to your calling because I've done exactly what you wanted me to do.'

▩ Food for thought

➢ Read 2 Corinthians 5:9,10.

➢ Spend time meditating on the phrase 'we make it our goal to please him'.

➢ List in a notebook everything you can think of which pleases God.

➢ How can *you* make it *your* goal to achieve what you have listed?

It was the bridegroom's tarrying that brought to light the state of the virgins ... Can we wait and still be ready? Some people can wait three days, but not three years. Some could hang on for three years ... but they may be required to watch for thirty. For consider this: if the bridegroom had come before midnight, all the virgins would have been wise! It was His delay which exposed their folly. May God preserve me from becoming foolish with the passing years!
Watchman Nee

▩ To seek

Spend time seeking God regarding the overall calling on your life, e.g. to be an evangelist, work with children, etc.

Set yourself some short-term goals to help you achieve your overall goal, e.g. I will be involved in Sunday School, church evangelism, etc.

❑ STUDY 14

Obstacles to prayer

If we confess our sins, he is faithful and just and will forgive us our sins and purify us from all unrighteousness (1 John 1:9).

(Abraham) did not waver through unbelief regarding the promise of God, but was strengthened in his faith and gave glory to God (Rom. 4:20).

Be very careful, then, how you live — not as unwise but as wise, making the most of every opportunity, because the days are evil (Eph. 5:15,16).

O Lord, open my lips, and my mouth will declare your praise (Ps. 51:15).

There are four main obstacles to an effective prayer life. The first two are spiritual; the other two, natural. Let's look at them.

Lack of confession. Prayer is no substitute for obedience. If you have unconfessed sin in your heart, there's no point in trying to bribe God with extra devotion. You need to repent and receive His forgiveness.

Lack of belief. God's Word tells us to 'pray continually' (1 Thess. 5:17). When you encounter delay or disappointment, it's easy to think, 'God isn't doing anything' and to give up. That's unbelief. Faith perseveres through trials and obtains what God has promised.

Lack of schedule. Some people fail to spend time with God simply because they don't write down a prayer schedule which suits their particular lifestyle. If you're zealous for God, you must organise your life — or others will do it for you. I can almost guarantee that if you have no schedule, you will probably pray very little on your own, but that if you do have one, you will probably be at least 60% faithful to it.

Free time always slips away if you're not jealous for it — those Saturday mornings when maybe you get up later, or Saturday nights

▩ To confess

If there is unconfessed sin in your life, confess it now and repent.

If you are ensnared by habitual sin go to someone you trust and ask them to help you.

▩ To meditate on

God wants our mouths to glorify Him.
'I will extol the LORD at all times; his praise will always be on my lips' (Ps. 34:1).
'My mouth will tell of your righteousness, of your salvation all day long ... I will come and proclaim your mighty acts ... to this day I declare your marvellous deeds' (Ps. 71:15a,16a,17b).
'I will sing of the LORD's great love for ever; with my mouth I will make your faithfulness known' (Ps. 89:1a).

when you feel at a loose end and do something just for the sake of it. Certainly I believe in the importance of family life and hospitality — but on many occasions we waste hours which we must redeem and use productively.

For a number of years my wife and I would go out for a quick Sunday lunch so that we could get back to the office and spend about four hours praying together. Throughout our married life we've had separate schedules and are accountable to one another for them. We've trained ourselves not to waste even the odd half hours — because they mount up.

Lack of vocabulary. Some people sort out their schedule but don't know how to express themselves to God. It takes time to acquire a vocabulary that communicates your feelings to Him. In family life, if you can express your love to your partner and children, you will find that your capacity for verbal appreciation actually increases. The same thing happens in your relationship with God. As you express your heart to Him, the Holy Spirit will give you more words and you will discover that you are actually able to pray for a very significant length of time.

▩ Food for thought

➢ Study the Lord's prayer (Matt. 6:9–13).

➢ Take each phrase and put it into your own words.

➢ Think about subjects for prayer which correspond to each phrase, e.g. give us this day our daily bread — personal needs, personal finance, world economy, poverty, famines, etc.

➢ Use this prayer as a framework, working through each phrase whenever you spend time in prayer.

▩ To organise

Organise your time for the coming week.

Schedule in time for prayer, worship, meditation, and silence (see Study 8).

Daily, disciplined prayer is one of the most difficult exercises Christians undertake.
Gordon MacDonald

❑ STUDY 15

Finding the words

I will pray with my spirit, but I will also pray with my mind (1 Cor. 14:15b).

How lovely is your dwelling-place, O LORD Almighty! My soul yearns, even faints for the courts of the LORD; my heart and my flesh cry out for the living God (Ps. 84:1,2).

We do not know what we ought to pray for, but the Spirit himself intercedes for us with groans that words cannot express. And he who searches our hearts knows the mind of the Spirit, because the Spirit intercedes for the saints in accordance with God's will (Rom. 8:26b,27).

I just want to comment again on the subject of prayer vocabulary. Some people say that they rely solely on the spontaneous inspiration of the Holy Spirit. Well, I've certainly had some tremendous seasons of Spirit-inspired prayer, but I've discovered that they don't always last. Often I find that a time of refreshing is followed by a period of dryness when God seems to hide Himself away. When this happens, where do you find the words to express your love to God?

I've discovered two ways. First, you can use the devotional Psalms (e.g. Ps. 8; 63; 65; 84). There are several of these and if you pray through them, they will inspire and motivate you. Second, you can use a prayer list — which I'd better explain.

When I was about eighteen I resolved to pray between 9.00 and 10.00 every night. After a while, I began to dread this hour because it was so hard to fill. I'd lock the door behind me, tell God I loved Him, thank Him for my parents, ask Him to bless the nations and think, 'I've still got 57 minutes to go!' Then I'd read and leave twenty minutes early feeling a failure.

Finally I began taking a notebook with me. Whenever I prayed something that seemed

▩ To discover

Make a list in a notebook of the benefits silence can bring to your personal devotions, using Scripture to illustrate where possible.

▩ To meditate on

God will help us to speak.
'Open wide your mouth and I will fill it' (Ps. 81:10b).
'Moses said to the LORD, "O Lord, I have never been eloquent, neither in the past nor since you have spoken to your servant. I am slow of speech and tongue." The LORD said to him, "Who gave man his mouth? ... Now go; I will help you speak and will teach you what to say"' (Exod. 4:10–12).

inspired, I'd write it down. At the end of a month I had a page of little sentences like, 'Lord, fill me with your love, put your power on me and help me to win the lost.' I'd then pray these things. The number of pages grew to about fifteen, and the time I needed to pray through them increased to over three hours.

So now, whenever I feel uninspired and wordless, I don't give up altogether, nor do I rely solely on the Spirit to give me the language I need. Instead, I return to my prayer list and pick up from where I left off the last time. Sometimes I'll be reading and praying the sentences back to the Lord for half an hour before a little spring breaks into the dryness. Then I'll let that current gradually take me into the presence of God.

Praying is about talking to a living Person. This means that you must be patient and make time for silence. I can spend anything from 10 seconds to 40 minutes on one paragraph or even one sentence in my prayer list. Sometimes I don't finish reading it. I just sit there quietly and consider the beauty of Jesus. I might pray in tongues or simply allow the Spirit to draw from me sighs of devotion and love.

▩ Food for thought

➢ Make a prayer list. Write down everything you want to pray for in a notebook, then divide the list into the days of the week.

Include in each day:

- the names of specific individuals
- a topic, e.g. the government, family life, revival, etc.

You may also want to have a separate list of people that you pray for every day.

➢ Put the lists into practice.

▩ To share

What do you talk about with your friends?

Do you share the same things when you are talking to the Lord?

What specific action can you take to share all of your life with the Lord?

When you pray, rather let your heart be without words than your words be without heart.
John Bunyan

❑ STUDY 16

Developing a prayer life

Hear my voice when I call, O LORD; be merciful to me and answer me. My heart says of you, 'Seek his face!' Your face, LORD, I will seek. Do not hide your face from me (Ps. 27:7–9a).

Do not be anxious about anything, but in everything, by prayer and petition, with thanksgiving, present your requests to God (Phil. 4:6).

And pray in the Spirit on all occasions with all kinds of prayers and requests. With this in mind, be alert and always keep on praying for all the saints (Eph. 6:18).

Finding a place to pray will be easy or hard depending on your circumstances. If it's difficult to get away from people where you live, don't give up. Instead, look for somewhere — an empty room at work or at college, maybe. You could even ask a Christian friend if you could use his flat. In winter you don't have to freeze to death on a park bench when you can use one of the public buildings. How about the local library or the coffee shop at the swimming baths? Don't let an apparent absence of a good location rob you of time with God.

The Bible tells us that we can engage in different kinds of prayer. I've divided the subject into four main categories — which aren't necessarily inspired! We'll be covering three of these elements over the next few days and the fourth — intercession both for the church and individuals — from Study 18.

Devotion. Worship underlines my devotional time. I refuse to race through my prayer list. Rather, I frequently interrupt my requests with expressions of thanksgiving, praise and adoration. I also worship God in tongues. Indeed, I would encourage anyone who doesn't have this gift to seek it, and anyone who

▩ To assess

Do you speak in tongues?

If not, spend time seeking the Lord for the gift. (If you have not been baptised in the Holy Spirit ask someone who has had this experience to pray for you.)

If you do speak in tongues do you frequently use this gift? Do you need to stir up the gift within you?

Spend 15 minutes praying in tongues.

▩ To meditate on

God listens when we pray.
'The eyes of the LORD are on the righteous and his ears are attentive to their cry' (Ps. 34:15).
'He fulfils the desires of those who fear him; he hears their cry and saves them' (Ps. 145:19).
'This is the confidence we have in approaching God: that if we ask anything according to his will, he hears us' (1 John 5:14).

doesn't use it much to use it more. The more you pray in tongues, the more you will appreciate its value in your devotional life.

Petition. When it comes to praying for myself, I focus first on God's goal for my life. And I talk through with Him things like fruitfulness, wisdom, gifts and worship. If I'm facing difficult circumstances, I ask God either to change them or to help me resolve them.

Meditation. Personal prayer and meditation tend to overlap. Sometimes I simply want to sit before the Lord and pour out my heart to Him. On other occasions I use the Bible as the basis for my prayers. God has had to correct me in the past — because I've spent too much time talking directly to Him when I should have been meditating on His Word.

Many people don't meditate on Scripture because they don't know where to begin. I suggest that you simply go to a particular book in the Bible and work your way through it systematically. It will help if you can buy or borrow a commentary so that if you come across something you don't understand, you can look it up. As you meditate, expect God to speak to you and to transform your life.

▩ Food for thought

➢ Read Ephesians 1:15–23.

➢ Paul's prayers give us an excellent pattern for our own prayer. Take each phrase and pray it for yourself. Use this pattern whenever you find it hard to know what to pray.

▩ To do

Start a prayer diary — write down what you pray for and when your prayer is answered. Note the date alongside the request.

As you see the answers to your prayers use them as a source of inspiration for times of thanksgiving and praise.

... we are taught, at the very outset of our search after the secret of effectual prayer, to remember that it is in the inner chamber, where we are alone with the Father, that we shall learn to pray aright.
Andrew Murray
With Christ in the School of Prayer

❑ **STUDY 17**

Meditate on the Word

The LORD would speak to Moses face to face, as a man speaks with his friend (Exod. 33:11a).

'I have called you friends' (John 15:15b).

'Search me, O God, and know my heart; test me and know my anxious thoughts. See if there is any offensive way in me, and lead me in the way everlasting' (Ps. 139:23,24).

When I meditate on the Scriptures, I don't allow myself to get bogged down by in-depth study because that's not my goal in my prayer times. My aim is not to gain intellectual insights but to engage in a dialogue with Jesus. So whatever I read I turn into conversation with the Lord.

I've discovered two kinds of Bible passage — faith and obedience. The faith passages encourage us to believe something. They speak about things like God's unconditional love for us, our righteousness in Christ, His goodness, faithfulness, justice, forgiveness and provision. When I'm meditating on a faith passage I thank God that what I'm reading is true — even if my emotions suggest otherwise. And I ask Him to give me fresh revelation of the particular promise that I'm reading about.

The obedience passages encourage us to do something and demand an active response. We are exhorted to reach out to the unsaved, heal the sick, offer hospitality, watch what we say, and so on. When I come to such a passage, I don't make vows or oaths to obey God, I simply tell Him that I will do what His Word says. I also allow the Holy Spirit to search my heart for

To consider

Which of God's promises do you find hardest to believe?

____

____

Read a passage that refers to this promise and pray for God's revelation to you.

To meditate on

Only God is qualified to judge us.
'The heart is deceitful above all things and beyond cure. Who can understand it? "I the LORD search the heart and examine the mind, to reward a man according to his conduct, according to what his deeds deserve"' (Jer. 17:9,10).
'If I do judge, my decisions are right, because I am not alone. I stand with the Father, who sent me' (John 8:16).

any personal failures which are revealed through my meditation.

I don't believe in morbid introspection. Certainly the Bible encourages us to examine ourselves, but it also tells us to fix our eyes on Jesus. If we turn our gaze inwards and strive endlessly to work out whether our motives were right or wrong, we will become very confused, insecure and depressed. Then, in our intense quest for inward spiritual perfection, we will lose sight of Jesus and the glory of His church.

We were not created to indulge in extensive self-analysis because we are not good enough judges of ourselves. If we are seeking the Lord and if our hearts are open to correction, Jesus will speak to us. I once doubted this. I thought that I might miss His voice and unconsciously continue to pursue a sinful course. But He challenged me to come to Him in faith and to believe that He would reveal Himself to me.

So now whenever I pray I keep my eyes fixed on Him rather than on my shortcomings. If I spend time worshipping Him and asking Him to speak to me, He will specifically pinpoint any failures. Then I will repent, thank Him for His forgiveness and ask Him to help me to obey.

▩ Food for thought

➢ Meditate on Psalm 1 and write down in a notebook the benefits of meditation.

➢ Over the next few days find out more about the practice of meditation. Read a book on the subject (e.g. *The Practice of Biblical Meditation* by Campbell McAlpine) or read through some chapters on meditation in a book about prayer (e.g. *Celebration of Discipline* by Richard Foster; *Listening to God* by Joyce Huggett; *Prayer: Key to Revival* by Paul Y. Cho).

▩ To resolve

We can spend most of our devotional time focusing on ourselves, our needs, our feelings, etc. and leave very little time for Jesus.

Resolve to reorientate your times with the Lord around Jesus. Leave praying for your own needs until after you have fixed your thoughts on Him through praise, thanksgiving, meditation, etc. Don't worry if you don't have enough time left for your list.

Meditation is the devotional practice of pondering the words of a verse, or verses of Scripture, with a receptive heart, allowing the Holy Spirit to take the written Word and apply it as the living Word to the inner being.
Campbell McAlpine

❑ STUDY 18

Not presumption but prayer

'I know your deeds, that you are neither cold nor hot. I wish you were either one or the other! So, because you are lukewarm — neither hot nor cold — I am about to spit you out of my mouth. You say, "I am rich; I have acquired wealth and do not need a thing." But you do not realise that you are wretched, pitiful, poor, blind and naked. I counsel you to buy from me gold refined in the fire, so that you can become rich; and white clothes to wear, so that you can cover your shameful nakedness; and salve to put on your eyes, so that you can see' (Rev. 3:15–18).

Someone once brought a significant prophetic dream to a church in America. In the dream God said, 'You think that you can do the work of the Kingdom without calling on me in prayer — and that's presumption.'

The Laodicean church was presumptuous. The people doubtless thought that their superb reputation would carry them along. Maybe they were keen to evangelise their city and had made plans to send out teams to spread the gospel. Whatever their intentions were, God saw through them and exposed the truth — they were living without reference to Him.

We can get very excited about the Kingdom of God. We can make great plans for expansion, erect bigger meeting places, train the entire congregation in evangelism and flood our streets with literature. But we cannot build the church if, behind all our zealous activity, we're not seeking the Lord.

Christians must intercede for the church. Gone are the days when we rely on the faithful prayers of half a dozen of our older members. If we're going to grow in maturity and in numbers every one of us must be whole-heartedly committed to cry out to God for breakthrough.

▒ To find

Find three examples of people who were presumptuous in the Bible.

____

____

____

What can you learn from each of these?

▒ To meditate on

God's people must pray and build. 'They all plotted together to come and fight against Jerusalem ... But we prayed to our God and ... continued the work' (Neh. 4:8a,9a,21a).

'"Now, Lord ... stretch out your hand to heal and perform miraculous signs and wonders through the name of your holy servant Jesus." After they prayed ... they were all filled with the Holy Spirit and spoke the word of God boldly' (Acts 4:29a,30,31a).

At the Kansas City Fellowship we have a model of intercession that I'd like to share with you in the next few studies. It's founded on six main premises.

1. Restoration of the church. It makes no sense to pray for something that you think is going to dwindle and die. If you assume that the church will go downhill before Jesus comes back, your prayers won't be motivated by faith and they won't have any impact. KCF are convinced that Jesus will return for a glorious church, so our prayers are full of expectation. We look forward to seeing a new move of God's Spirit among His people and the manifestation of His power in signs and wonders.

2. Unified churches. We believe that God wants to bring about a unified expression of His church in various locations. By this we mean that a team of elders will oversee one particular group of churches in a large area and that this pattern will be multiplied across the nation.

3. Regular corporate intercession. We're convinced that corporate intercession is essential for growth, so we have three regular prayer meetings every day. We want to be found guilty of prayerfulness, not presumption.

▩ Food for thought

➢ Read through Acts 2—5.

➢ Write down in a notebook the characteristics of the New Testament church.

➢ Which, if any, of these features is missing from your church? Why do you think that is?

➢ What do you understand by the term 'the restoration of the church'?

▩ To consider

Is there enough corporate prayer in your local church? If not, what could you do about it?

Do you personally spend enough time praying for the church?

List six areas of church life which you can pray for on a regular basis.

____

____

The basic truth about prayer is that God is even more ready to listen than we are to speak to him, and even more ready to give than we are to ask.
David Hanes

❑ STUDY 19

Jerusalem first

(Jesus) told them, 'This is what is written: The Christ will suffer and rise from the dead on the third day, and repentance and forgiveness of sins will be preached in his name to all nations, beginning at Jerusalem' (Luke 24:46,47).

'But you will receive power when the Holy Spirit comes on you; and you will be my witnesses in Jerusalem, and in all Judea and Samaria, and to the ends of the earth' (Acts 1:8).

The fourth premise in our Kansas City model of responsibility in intercession is this: **we begin praying for our own locality before we reach out to other places**. It's 'Jerusalem' first.

Early in my ministry I used to pray a lot for the nations. Then God challenged me about it. 'Why are you praying for other cities when your own city is completely barren?' He asked. Then He pointed me to Acts 1:8 and I received a fresh revelation of the pattern that He'd given to the first-century church.

Now I'm not saying that it's unbiblical to pray for the nations. Far from it. Paul prayed for the Philippians and the Thessalonians. So if God gives you a burden for a specific country or two, then you must obey His leading. It's just that you will find it hard to cry out to God for places if you have no real heart for them.

Some people's prayers are actually motivated by guilt. 'I ought to be concerned for missionary work,' they think. 'So I'd better give a five-minute shot to China.' They may appease their guilt, but their prayers won't do much because faith doesn't lie behind them.

I'm no longer interested in scattering shotgun prayers around the world because I don't have

▩ To discover

Think about your immediate locality and write down in a notebook some of the main prayer needs, e.g. local government, single mums, housing estates, etc.

Find out about any organisations which are seeking to help in these areas and pray for them.

▩ To meditate on

Faith is essential to prayer.
'According to your faith will it be done to you' (Matt. 9:29b).
'If anyone says to this mountain, "Go, throw yourself into the sea," and does not doubt in his heart but believes that what he says will happen, it will be done for him ... whatever you ask for in prayer, believe that you have received it, and it will be yours' (Mark 11:23,24).
'Everything that does not come from faith is sin' (Rom. 14:23b).

confidence in them. I look at the minimal results that we've had from thousands of hours of intercession for KC and I think, 'A five-minute blast for China isn't going to make that much impact.' And my low faith level naturally hinders the effectiveness of my prayers.

Church leaders must put restraints on their prayer focus or they'll lose the support of their people. It's no good thinking, 'God loves China. Let's start asking Him to bless the Chinese.' You may get a reasonable turnout for the first prayer meeting but as time goes on, numbers will start to fall because in reality the people have no heart for that nation.

At KC we set prayer boundaries and spend 85 per cent of our corporate prayer meetings calling on God for the outpouring of the Spirit on our own area. When we see a significant increase in numbers, maybe we'll start believing God for Chicago and then for other areas. It depends how He directs us.

So, as a general rule, pray first for your own town or city and when you see God move there, believe Him for regions further away. Pray within your faith. Unless the Lord is building your prayer focuses, you will labour in vain.

▩ Food for thought

➢ Read 2 Corinthians 10:13–16.

➢ What do you understand by the following phrases:

- the field God has assigned to us?
- our area of activity?
- another man's territory?

➢ Did Paul's boundaries in any way limit the scope and scale of his ministry?

▩ To pray

Seek God about whether He wants to give you a specific prayer burden for a particular country or group of people, e.g. local government, single mums, the elderly, housing estates, schools, etc.

Be attentive to His answer over the next few days.

When God's people use the weapon of prayer, they are not trapped by rising or lowering trends, but take part in shaping the history of their local area.
Kjell Sjöberg

❑ STUDY 20

Come, Holy Spirit!

'If you then, though you are evil, know how to give good gifts to your children, how much more will your Father in heaven give the Holy Spirit to those who ask him!' (Luke 11:13)

God is not a God of disorder but of peace (1 Cor. 14:33).

I believe that the church's greatest prayer is for the **outpouring of the Spirit on a geographical area**. That's premise number 5.

If there isn't a sense of agreement about the direction in which your church is headed, you will end up with people bringing their own burdens to the prayer meeting. At KC we encourage individuals to use the microphone so you can imagine the chaos that would ensue if there were no clear boundary lines. Brother Bill would be up there at the front getting carried away over the starving millions in Ethiopia and Sister Sue would be thinking, 'What's he praying that for? He's just showing off.'

After about six months of this kind of thing, numbers will probably have dropped to the faithful ten or twelve. That's not because the rest dislike prayer. It's just because they can't cope with the liberty. There's no clear sense of purpose, nothing to spur them on, no overall faith goal to motivate them to attend.

So at KC we don't focus our corporate prayers on individual needs, we ask God to rend the heavens and come in power. Then we spend a short time praying for specific requests as the leader feels appropriate. We could invest

▩ To question

Read Joel 2:28–32.

What are the features of an outpouring of the Holy Spirit?

____

____

Think about individuals you regularly pray for. How would their needs be met by such an outpouring?

▩ To meditate on

God encourages us to plan.
'Plans fail for lack of counsel, but with many advisers they succeed' (Prov. 15:22).
'Make plans' (Prov. 20:18a).
'The noble man makes noble plans ... by noble deeds he stands' (Isa. 32:8).
'Paul decided to go to Jerusalem, passing through Macedonia and Achaia' (Acts 19:21a).
'Each man should give what he has decided in his heart' (2 Cor. 9:7a).

10,000 hours interceding for individuals, but we feel that the time is better spent crying to God for an area — because when He sends His Spirit, many individual needs will also be met.

Isn't that what happened at Pentecost? The Spirit fell on Jerusalem and thousands were saved. Then they started selling things and giving the money to those in need, and praying for people and seeing them healed.

We're not into corporate 'pea shooter' prayers which frighten the enemy away from a few individuals for a while. We're looking for God to blast all His artillery against the kingdom of darkness and to conquer mighty strongholds to the glory of His name.

I'm convinced that God is going to visit us with great power. We're going to sense His presence in an amazing way; see thousands of conversions; witness incredible miracles and reach out to the needy with deeper love than ever before. It's this that stirs me more than corporate prayer for individuals. But I know that the power will come only in response to the fervent and persistent intercession of people who believe that God will give the Holy Spirit to those who ask Him.

Food for thought

➢ Get hold of a book on a revival, e.g. *The Hebridean Revival.*

➢ Particularly notice what happened when the Holy Spirit came with power.

➢ Re-read these passages frequently and let them inspire you to pray for revival.

To challenge

In what ways are you reaching out to the needy?

Should you be doing more?

Pray about this and ask the Lord to show you what He wants you to do.

The history of revivals, both ancient and more recent, clearly indicates one overriding factor common to all of them — prayer. Nothing was accomplished of any significance except that the people of God first got serious about the matter of seeking God.
Floyd McClung

❑ STUDY 21

A spirit of prayer

'I will pour out on the house of David and the inhabitants of Jerusalem a spirit of grace and supplication' (Zech. 12:10a).

Through (Jesus) we ... have access to the Father by one Spirit (Eph. 2:18).

They all joined together constantly in prayer, along with the women and Mary the mother of Jesus, and with his brothers (Acts 1:14; 2:1a).

The last premise for intercession is our conviction that **God is going to pour a spirit of prayer on His church**.

By this, I'm not talking about general faithfulness in prayer or about a bit of emotion and a few tears. I'm referring to supernaturally inspired travail and groaning for the lost. The Spirit will come on the church, we will enter deeply into Christ's prayers and our hearts will be broken for those who don't know Him.

Some people are so impatient for this visitation that they neglect normal prayer. Their meetings are geared to 'getting into the place where God can release His spirit of prayer among us'. They change their methods in anticipation of this great event, and focus almost exclusively on thanksgiving, praise and worship — but not on earnest, persevering prayer. I'm not surprised when, four months later, the gatherings have ceased to exist.

There are other meetings where people have almost tried to manipulate a new experience of prayer. They weep, wail and gush with energetic and dramatic supplications, but the Spirit doesn't fall and set their hearts on fire. A month later, things haven't changed, and after

▩ To answer

What is God saying to you about:

- your attendance at prayer meetings?
- your faithfulness in prayer?

▩ To meditate on

God has a time for everything.
'I will return to you at the appointed time next year and Sarah will have a son' (Gen. 18:14b).
'Jesus replied, "My time has not yet come"' (John 2:4b).
'Father, the time has come. Glorify your Son' (John 17:1b).
'It is not for you to know the times or dates the Father has set by his own authority' (Acts 1:7b).

five years there's still no evidence of a mighty breakthrough of supernatural power.

I'm all in favour of zeal and emotion in the prayer meeting, but you can't convince me that a spirit of supplication has come when it hasn't. In past revivals, you knew when the Spirit of God had descended — not because there were people earnestly praying and crying, but because He pervaded the atmosphere. It was an awesome experience.

The spirit of prayer will come — in God's time. When He does move, you won't have to drag people to the prayer meeting — they'll be on the doorstep hours beforehand. It's easy to attend something when the power of God is breaking out; it's more difficult when nothing supernatural seems to be happening and when prayer seems to be a constant battle.

We aren't asking God for lively meetings. We're seeking Him for a life-changing visitation that will transform nations. God looks for those who are faithful without the anointing. They're people who are committed to the meetings because they love God, and because they want to be involved in bringing about His blessing rather than just enjoying it when it comes.

▩ Food for thought

➢ Read Psalms 18:25; 31:23; 37:28; 97:10; 101:6; Proverbs 2:8; 3:3,4; 28:20; Matthew 25:21.

➢ How does God reward faithfulness? Write down the areas in which God wants us to be faithful.

▩ To analyse

Do you find that corporate or personal prayer is a constant battle?

Write down in a notebook why you think this is. Analyse your reasons and make any practical adjustments to your lifestyle, etc. which will help you.

Talk to the Lord about your difficulties and ask Him to help you overcome them.

To be a spiritual intercessor, we must have a desire to stand in the gap. Intercessor literally means to stand between. We must be willing to stand between the need and God, the only One able to meet the need.
Paul Y. Cho

❑ STUDY 22

Be foolish to be wise

If any one of you thinks he is wise by the standards of this age, he should become a 'fool' so that he may become wise (1 Cor. 3:18b).

The news about (Jesus) spread ... so that crowds of people came to hear him and to be healed of their sicknesses. But Jesus often withdrew to lonely places and prayed (Luke 5:15,16).

We always thank God for all of you, mentioning you in our prayers. We continually remember before our God and Father your work ... your labour ... and your endurance (1 Thess. 1:2,3a).

For about ten years God pulled me out of a great deal of ministry. 'You really want to fulfil your destiny, don't you?' He said. 'Right, I want you to sit in that room for several hours a day and pray back to me what I tell you. As you do that, principalities will be subdued and my power will be released.'

I couldn't understand the logic of this. Here I was, turning down speaking opportunities in order to relate back to God what He passed on to me! I was even more puzzled when He began encouraging me to fast as well. How could praying and not eating establish the Kingdom of God? The whole idea seemed ludicrous.

To the carnal mind, intercession is foolish, but not to God — and not to those who realise that His wisdom is far superior to theirs. The apostle Paul spent hours praying, and he became the most powerful and successful Christian who has ever lived. He submitted to God's foolish wisdom, and God made Him great.

My rational mind questions, 'Why does Jesus always live to intercede for us (Heb. 7:25b)? If He's God, then why is God praying to God!?' The only way I can make sense of this is to

▩ To understand

Reason is much esteemed in today's world but what place does it have in the life of a Christian?

What are its advantages?

___

What are its disadvantages?

___

▩ To meditate on

God searches for wise people.
'God looks down from heaven on the sons of men to see if there are any who understand, any who seek God' (Ps. 53:2).
'I looked for a man ... who would build up the wall and stand before me in the gap on behalf of the land so that I would not have to destroy it, but I found none' (Ezek. 22:30).

apply God's wisdom and bow to it. If Jesus is interceding for us, it must be a relevant activity. So I will engage in it too.

I can't say that intercession is easy. It's not. On the odd occasion I find it exhilarating, but not for the majority of the time. Usually it's hard work — sometimes mundane, sometimes even boring. But whatever my personal feelings about it, I will still pray. I can think of nothing better to do than imitate Jesus.

Scripture says, '[God] was astonished that there was no one to intercede' (Isa. 59:16b NASB). I believe that today God is searching for intercessors. He sees a lot of believers who are doing OK in their Christian lives, but not many who are willing to submit whole-heartedly to His wisdom. He's looking for people who don't conform to logic; people who frequently draw away from legitimate activities in order to pray; people whose hearts are motivated by eternal values which supersede those on earth.

What will happen as Christians start submitting to God's wisdom and praying like His Son? Surely they will manifest the same breathtaking power as Jesus, and the church will rise up and give great glory to His name.

▩ Food for thought

➢ Read 1 Corinthians 1:18–31.

➢ In two columns write down in a notebook a comparison of worldly wisdom and so called 'foolishness'.

➢ What are the results of each of these? What does this tell you about worldly wisdom? What does it tell you about our attitude towards being seen to be foolish?

▩ To investigate

From the Bible write down six apparently illogical things that God/Jesus told people to do.

____

____

____

If God told you to do something that seemed illogical would you be prepared to do it?

God is sovereign, He can do whatever He wishes, but He has chosen to work in response to the prayers of His people.
Ian Christensen

❑ STUDY 23

Give Him no rest

I have posted watchmen on your walls, O Jerusalem; they will never be silent day or night. You who call on the LORD, give yourselves no rest, and give him no rest till he establishes Jerusalem and makes her the praise of the earth (Isa. 62:6–7).

... always keep on praying for all the saints (Eph. 6:18b).

'Will not God bring about justice for his chosen ones, who cry out to him day and night?' (Luke 18:7a)

I am not one of those people who think that all God's promises to Israel should be given to the church. Rather, I have a very strong commitment to God's purposes for the Jews and I know that many of His words have not yet been fulfilled for them. So when I read Isaiah 62:6–7, I interpret it to refer primarily to the natural Jerusalem, although I do feel that it can apply to those who belong to the spiritual Jerusalem as well.

The verses from Isaiah explain the activity of the 'watchmen'. God appoints these people to a more specific prayer ministry than other believers — although He still expects every Christian to pray earnestly for the church. Sometimes the watchmen are intercessors; sometimes they're prophets. And often the two roles overlap.

God's mandate for an intercessor is this: to call on Him day and night until He establishes His purposes on earth. I believe that the words 'day and night' are literal. Paul prayed 'night and day' for the Thessalonians (1 Thess. 3:10) and God wants the members of every local church not to give themselves or Him any rest until He comes in power.

▩ To seek

Spend time seeking the Lord about whether or not you have a specific call to intercession or to be a 'watchman'.

Be open to hearing *whatever* the Lord has to say to you.

▩ To meditate on

We need to feel the intercessor's heart. '"Those who survived the exile ... are in great trouble ... The wall of Jerusalem is broken down, and its gates have been burned with fire." When I heard these things, I sat down and wept. For some days I mourned and fasted and prayed' (Neh. 1:3,4).

'My eyes fail from weeping, I am in torment within, my heart is poured out on the ground because my people are destroyed' (Lam. 2:11a).

Some people might question, 'Does that mean that if I don't pray, God's plans will be thwarted and He won't visit us?' And I would reply, 'No. It doesn't mean that at all. God is sovereign and your disobedience won't abort His plans. If you refuse to pray, the works that He has ordained for you will be done through the faithful prayers of others.'

A number of believers want some sort of spiritual experience before they intercede for the church. 'I'll pray when I receive a vision or a prophecy about it,' they say. But God looks for obedience whether or not we're given some supernatural sign. He has told us to pray in His Word. Further spiritual revelation about this should therefore be totally unnecessary. Either we choose to obey, or we don't.

God searches for watchmen who will give Him no rest until He establishes His Kingdom on the earth. He's looking for people who are motivated not by guilt, but by grace — people who realise that it's a high privilege to labour alongside Him in His eternal purposes. On the day He visits them in power, they will rejoice to know that He was responding to their own prayers rather than to the prayers of others.

▩ Food for thought

➢ Read 1 Corinthians 1:4–9; 3:14–19; Philippians 1:3–11; Colossians 1:3–14; 3:9–13; 5:23; 2 Thessalonians 1:3; 2:13, 16–17; 3:16.

➢ Study the way Paul prayed for these churches.

➢ Incorporate these themes when you pray for the church.

▩ To review

How important are 'spiritual experiences' in receiving guidance?

Are you 'waiting for a sign' in some area of your life? If so, go back to the Word and discover what it has to say on the subject.

If not, review whether or not you are being obedient to the Word in every way.

Pray often, for prayer is a shield to the soul, a sacrifice to God, and a scourge to Satan.
John Bunyan

❑ STUDY 24

Perceive and intercede

'Forget the former things; do not dwell on the past. See, I am doing a new thing! Now it springs up; do you not perceive it? I am making a way in the desert and streams in the wasteland ... Yet you have not called upon me, O Jacob, you have not wearied yourselves for me, O Israel. You have not brought me sheep for burnt offerings, nor honoured me with your sacrifices ... But you have burdened me with your sins and wearied me with your offences. I, even I, am he who blots out your transgressions, for my own sake, and remembers your sins no more. Review the past for me, let us argue the matter together; state the case for your innocence'
(See Isa. 43:18–26).

Churches in every part of the world have recently been receiving the same prophetic word from God: 'Forget the former things. I'm doing something new among you.' Those people who are sensitive to God don't need Him to ask them, 'Don't you perceive it?' They're all too aware that He's patiently at work behind the scenes and are looking forward with great expectation and excitement to the breakthrough of His power in the world arena.

Clearly Isaiah 43 applies mainly to the nation of Israel, but Christians can learn something from the Jews' pathetic response to God. They should have been caught up in His purposes, but seemed to be totally indifferent to what He was doing and refused to be part of it.

God told His people that He was going to 'make a way in the desert and streams in the wasteland'. This promise was figurative, not literal. It revealed the amazing manner in which God was going to bless His people. Water doesn't usually burst up and flow through a desert, so when God used this analogy to describe His plan for Israel, He was effectively saying, 'I'm going to release my supernatural power and do something totally dynamic.'

▩ To ask

'Men of Issachar, who understood the times and knew what Israel should do' (1 Chron. 12:32a).

Do you understand the times and what God is doing on the earth today?

Ask the Lord to give you revelation. The closer you draw to Him the more sensitive to God you will become.

▩ To meditate on

Let's pray earnestly for our nation.
'If my people, who are called by my name, will humble themselves and pray and seek my face and turn from their wicked ways, then will I hear from heaven and will forgive their sin and will heal their land' (2 Chr. 7:14).
'I turned to the Lord God and pleaded with him in prayer and petition, in fasting, and in sackcloth and ashes' (Dan. 9:3).

What He wanted His people to do was catch this vision, get behind it and pray it into existence. He was inviting them to labour alongside Him in the outworking of a mighty breakthrough in their nation. What did they do? They heard His prophetic word but simply ignored it and carried on sinning. Earnest 'day and night' prayer was far from their minds. They were stuck in meaningless religious rituals and neither called on Him nor wearied themselves for His sake.

Intercession begins with repentance. Isaiah's prophecy continues with God reminding Israel that He could forgive them and inviting them to 'state the case for your innocence'. In other words, 'Let's argue this out together. I'm calling you to repent and then to give me a good reason why I should move in power on the earth.'

That's what intercession is all about — wrestling with God to fulfil His plans. If we want revival, the church must respond to this invitation to intercede. In every nation we must cry out to Him, 'Father, we have sinned but you are merciful. Forgive our sin. Release your power in this barren nation. Send times of refreshing from the presence of the Lord.'

▩ Food for thought

➢ Read Genesis 18:16–23; Nehemiah 1 and 9; Daniel 9.

➢ What are the hallmarks of these intercessory prayers?

➢ Using these prayers as a guide write out an intercessory prayer on behalf of the nation, or your church.

▩ To repent

Repentance indicates that you mean business with God.

Take stock of your life and repent of anything that you know to be ungodly — bad attitudes, specific sin, apathy, etc.

Tell the Lord that you do mean business and begin to intercede regularly for your nation.

O breath of life, come
sweeping through us,
Revive thy church with life
and power;
O breath of life, come
cleanse, renew us,
And fit thy church to meet
this hour.
Mrs B. P. Head
'O breath of life'

❑ STUDY 25

O Lord, remember

Awake, awake! Clothe yourself with strength, O arm of the LORD; awake, as in days gone by, as in generations of old. Was it not you who cut Rahab to pieces, who pierced that monster through? Was it not you who dried up the sea, the waters of the great deep, who made a road in the depths of the sea so that the redeemed might cross over? The ransomed of the LORD will return. They will enter Zion with singing; everlasting joy will crown their heads. Gladness and joy will overtake them, and sorrow and sighing will flee away (Isa. 51:9–11).

O LORD, remember David and all the hardships he endured (Ps. 132:1).

The theme of 'reminding the Lord' plays a very important part in intercession. When Bible characters earnestly cried out to God, they reminded Him of two things: His acts in history and His promises.

In Isaiah 51:9–11 we see Isaiah reminding God of His acts in history. When Isaiah prayed to the Lord, 'Awake, as in days gone by,' he wasn't assuming that God was literally asleep. Rather, he was looking around at the lack of spiritual breakthrough in the nation and calling on God to take action and manifest His power — just as He had in the past.

The prophet directed God's attention to the early days when He performed mighty miracles for His people. The word 'Rahab' was probably a reference to Egypt (Isa. 30:7). So here Isaiah was focusing on God's amazing deliverance of His people from captivity and prophesying a glorious future release for them.

In the same way, God wants us to remind Him of His wonderful works — particularly in the New Testament. 'Awake, Lord!' we say to Him. 'Remember the day when you delivered us from sin through the sacrifice of Jesus on the cross. Recall the signs and wonders that He

▩ To compare

Compare Psalm 121:3 with John 5:16,17.

What important truth do these verses reveal about the Lord?

____

____

How can this motivate you to pray?

▩ To meditate on

Jesus will inherit the nations.
'He said to me, "You are my Son ... Ask of me, and I will make the nations your inheritance, the ends of the earth your possession"' (Ps. 2:7b,8).
'The Lord God will give him the throne of his father David, and ... his kingdom will never end' (Luke 1:32b,33b).
'The kingdom of the world has become the kingdom of our Lord and of his Christ, and he will reign for ever and ever' (Rev. 11:15b).

performed. Look back at the early church — you sent your Spirit and thousands were saved, and you gave them such power! Do the same for us. We want to see the blind seeing and the crippled walking. Visit us again, O God!'

When the Psalmist declared, 'O LORD, remember David' (Ps. 132:1a), he was appealing to a great promise that God had made, namely that David's throne would be established for ever and ever (Ps. 132:11,12,17,18). The early Christians realised that this promise was fulfilled in Jesus and reminded God about it in prayer when they quoted from a recognised Messianic psalm (Acts 4:23–31).

God's eternal purpose is to give the nations to His Son as an inheritance. When we pray along the lines, 'Your kingdom come!' we're effectively saying, 'O Lord, remember Jesus. Bring to mind your great plan. You said that a multitude from 'every tribe and language and people and nation' would come to Him (Rev. 5:9,10) and that He would rule as their King for ever and ever. I believe that you will fulfil your word. Recall your promise. Establish the throne of your Son. Make the name of Jesus great in all the earth.'

Food for thought

➢ Re-read Nehemiah 1 and 9. In a notebook list in two columns:

- the past acts of God
- His promises.

➢ Read Psalm 77:11. Taking ideas from your answers in the first column, record some of the things that God has done for you.

➢ Write down any personal promises which God has made to you and pray for their fulfilment.

To understand

When we ask God to remember, we are not asking Him to reminisce with nostalgia about the good old days but to urge Him to fulfil His promises in our time.

Begin to focus on God's promises in your intercession. Let faith rise in your heart as you picture what it will be like when God fulfils His Word.

Do you argue your case before God? We need to pray, 'Lord you have promised,' so that we plead the promises as our way to receive mighty answers. He is a covenant-keeping God with whom we may dare to argue.
Terry Virgo

❑ STUDY 26

Wanted: Radical Christians

I went past the field of the sluggard, past the vineyard of the man who lacks judgment; thorns had come up everywhere, the ground was covered with weeds, and the stone wall was in ruins. I applied my heart to what I observed and learned a lesson from what I saw: A little sleep, a little slumber, a little folding of the hands to rest — and poverty will come on you like a bandit and scarcity like an armed man (Prov. 24:30–34).

Too many believers simply live to enjoy themselves. Their motto is 'lie back and take it easy' — which is exactly what they do.

They don't necessarily dabble in blatantly sinful practices. It's more a sort of focus on personal desires. They have that carefree attitude which says things like, 'I deserve my free time, and since I've got a natural weakness for the beach, that's where you'll find me every weekend.' You could be tempted to envy their apparent freedom to do as they like — until you see how directionless their lives really are.

Others of us aren't quite so self-indulgent. Indeed, we might even cast a quick sideways glance at the 'lazy Christians' and come to the conclusion, 'I'm much more radical than they are.' Then one day we read about the activities of some of the godly men and women in the past and realise that we've been totally self-deceived. Their love for God and zeal for His Kingdom put us to shame and change our self-assessment to 'lukewarm'.

Several years ago God spoke to me about my being someone of whom the world was not worthy (Heb. 11:38). 'Why do you leave whole-hearted commitment to the David Brainerds,

▩ To define

Write down a definition of what it means to be radical, giving examples from everyday life to illustrate your definition.

____

____

____

____

▩ To meditate on

Zeal manifests itself in action.
'Phineas ... will have a covenant of a lasting priesthood, because he was zealous for the honour of his God' (See Num. 25:1–13).
'(David) swore an oath to the LORD and made a vow to the Mighty One of Jacob: "I will not enter my house or go to my bed — I will allow no sleep to my eyes, no slumber to my eyelids, till I find a place for the LORD, a dwelling for the Mighty One of Jacob"' (Ps. 132:2–5).

Martin Luthers and John Wesleys?' He said. 'What's to prevent you from being just like them? Why don't you set a model of radical Christianity for others to follow?'

God is saying a similar thing to Christians today. 'Are you content to be like other people?' He asks. 'Do you really think that you'll find fulfilment in personal happiness and worldly pleasures? Or will you see that I have a far greater and more satisfying purpose for your life? Will you give yourself to a passing age or to an eternal Kingdom?'

If we don't have anything to die for, we don't have anything to live for either. It's not worth living or dying for anything in the world. But it's worth living and dying for Jesus. Radical Christianity is a costly, all-consuming thing. It means that we stop concentrating on ourselves and begin focusing on the Kingdom of heaven.

God searches for men and women who aren't afraid to be radical, people who say, 'Lord, I don't care if others ridicule me for my desire to be more committed to you. And I waive all my rights and privileges. From now on I have only one consuming passion and that's to see Jesus glorified in the earth.' Are you radical?

Food for thought

➢ Read a Christian biography this month.

➢ As you do so write down in a notebook any characteristics you aspire to. Talk to the Lord about them and ask Him to help you make changes in your own life.

To challenge

Can you genuinely apply the final paragraph of the main text to yourself?

If not, identify any obstacles to this and ask the Lord to help you overcome them.

It is only as we willingly embrace the cross that the axe is laid to the root of all within us that is opposed to the deep working of the Holy Spirit.
Arthur Wallis

❑ STUDY 27

Discipline and persistence

Then Jesus told his disciples a parable to show them that they should always pray and not give up. He said: 'In a certain town there was a judge who neither feared God nor cared about men. And there was a widow in that town who kept coming to him with the plea, "Grant me justice against my adversary." For some time he refused. But finally he said to himself, "Even though I don't fear God or care about men, yet because this widow keeps bothering me, I will see that she gets justice, so that she won't eventually wear me out with her coming!"' (Luke 18:1–5)

Jesus tells us that we should 'always pray and not give up'. The human spirit was created to commune with God and to cry out for His purposes to be fulfilled in the earth. Sadly, some people's hearts are dull and hard. These individuals have tried to survive without much dialogue with God and, like unwatered plants, they've wilted inside.

They may be so afraid of getting bound up in ritualism that they've totally avoided regular spiritual activities. 'I'm terrified of falling into legalism,' they think. 'So I'll play safe and steer clear of rigid patterns of behaviour. I can still be radical — even if I may not be too prayerful.'

Wise Christians don't avoid legalism by drifting into licence but by embracing discipline. They're motivated by grace and love for God. 'I'm really keen to spend time in His presence every day,' they say. 'So I'm happy to discipline my life to make that possible. And if Jesus wants me to fast for 24 hours or so each week, I know it will be hard, but I'll willingly do it for His sake.' Dutiful slaves feel that they *have* to obey; liberated sons *want* to do so.

The parable of the widow and the unjust judge highlights the need not just for prayer,

▩ To identify

What is God saying to you about your devotional life, i.e. more regularity, fasting, etc.?

____

____

____

What response do you need to make to this?

▩ To meditate on

God loves a prevailing spirit.
'Jacob was left alone, and a man wrestled with him ... the man said, "Let me go, for it is daybreak." But Jacob replied, "I will not let you go unless you bless me"' (Gen. 32:24,26).
'The LORD said to Moses, "... they are a stiff-necked people. Now leave me alone so that ... I may destroy them ..." But Moses sought the favour of the LORD his God' (Exod. 32:9b,10a,11a).

but for persistence in it. We might question why one prayer often isn't sufficient for God to act. He has His own reasons, but one of them may be that He's as keen to develop our faith while we ask as He is to answer our request.

Hand in hand with the cry for the outpouring of God's Spirit goes a cry for justice. Day after day God sees the exploitation of 'innocent' people and longs to put right the wrongs that are being done to them. He could easily step in and rescue them without the help of believers, but He has decided to limit His activity and to respond only to fervent prayer.

When you want something enough, you'll do almost anything to get it. God is deeply concerned about justice. He's not looking for people who will merely offer a few casual prayers on the subject. He's longing to see His passion in our hearts and to hear us 'cry out to Him day and night' for victory over oppression and the establishment of righteousness.

The widow was rewarded for her persistence. Many Christians pray but don't prevail. They fail to grasp God's promise — that if they persist, He will 'see that they get justice, and quickly' (Luke 18:8a).

Food for thought

➢ Read Isaiah 58.

➢ Make a point of reading your local newspaper regularly. Pray about any injustice you find in it.

➢ Ask the Lord if He wants you to be personally involved in helping those facing injustice.

To analyse

Are you a casual pray-er?

Do you care enough about anything to give yourself in prayer for it?

Ask God to reveal to you how He feels about the lost, the oppressed or the church. Feel His passion and let it spur you to cry out to God.

Work as if everything depended upon your work, and pray as if everything depended upon your prayer.
General William Booth

❑ STUDY 28

Grace awakening

Through (Jesus) we have gained access by faith into this grace in which we now stand (Rom. 5:2).

If, by the trespass of the one man, death reigned through that one man, how much more will those who receive God's abundant provision of grace ... reign in life through the one man, Jesus Christ (Rom. 5:17).

With great power the apostles continued to testify to the resurrection of the Lord Jesus, and much grace was upon them all (Acts 4:33).

As we pray for the outpouring of the Spirit on our area, we're effectively asking God to give us a fresh revelation of His grace.

Grace has been defined as the free unmerited favour of God. A sinner abandons his attempts to earn salvation by pleasing God and receives by faith the gift of eternal life (Rom. 6:23b). We are saved not by works through intelligence but 'by grace ... through faith' (Eph. 2:8).

Grace enables us to 'reign in life'. Now many Christians would say that they were 'battling' rather than 'reigning'. They aren't experiencing the riches of God's grace because they've returned to good works in an attempt to satisfy God. We reign not by striving but by 'receiving'. He has given us an abundant provision of grace and wants us to enter it and experience His victory over sin and condemnation.

The apostle Peter also refers to our having grace 'in abundance' (1 Pet. 1:2b). After the outpouring of the Spirit at Pentecost, the church was full of power and grace. God wants us to know His power in us; He also wants us to enjoy His grace. The Spirit has 'lavished' God's grace on us (Eph. 1:8); we must grow and be strong in it (2 Pet. 3:18a; 2 Tim. 2:1b).

▩ To pray

Spend time asking God for a fresh revelation of His grace.

In particular ask the Lord to help you apply this wonderful gift in your own life — especially in areas where you are battling.

▩ To meditate on

Grace should affect conduct.
'(God's) grace to me was not without effect. No, I worked harder than all of them — yet not I, but the grace of God that was with me' (1 Cor. 15:10b)
'Not according to worldly wisdom but according to God's grace' (2 Cor. 1:12b).
'Excel in this grace of giving' (2 Cor. 8:7b).
'Let your conversation be always full of grace' (Col. 4:6a).

God invites us to 'approach the throne of grace with confidence, so that we may receive mercy and find grace to help us in our time of need' (Heb. 4:16). And James says, 'he gives us more grace ... God ... gives grace to the humble' (James 4:6b). The greater our needs, the greater is God's supply of the grace to meet them. Humble people acknowledge their dependence on Him and willingly receive from Him all that's necessary for their salvation.

The apostle Paul received grace to preach Christ and to reveal God's hidden plans (Eph. 3:8,9). God will give you grace for whatever task He has called you to do. You may think that you haven't got the strength to accomplish His purposes, but His grace will always be sufficient for you to get the job done.

Paul said, 'The grace of our Lord was poured out on me abundantly' (1 Tim. 1:14a). What we want to see when we cry out to God for revival is the reign of grace in the life of every believer. I encourage people to pray for grace to be manifested in wisdom, fruitfulness and power. We need a deep awareness of the way that the Spirit is moving among us, godly character and signs and wonders to confirm the Word.

Food for thought

➢ Read 2 Corinthians 13:13. Now write down in your notebook what each phrase of this verse means.

➢ What a powerful prayer this is! Use it not as 'mindless repetition' but as a prayer of faith.

To assess

Write down all that grace means to you in your life.

____

____

____

____

Give thanks to God for all that He's done for you.

Grace first inscribed my name,
In God's eternal book:
'Twas grace that gave me to the Lamb
Who all my sorrows took.

Grace taught my soul to pray,
And pardoning love to know;
'Twas grace that kept me to this day,
And will not let me go.
Doddridge

❑ STUDY 29

Pray for wisdom

(God) 'gives wisdom to the wise and knowledge to the discerning. He reveals deep and hidden things' (Dan. 2:21b,22a).

Surely the Sovereign LORD does nothing without revealing his plan to his servants the prophets (Amos 3:7).

He who forms the mountains, creates the wind, and reveals his thoughts to man (Amos 4:13a).

God wants to reveal His manifold wisdom through the church to the rulers and authorities in the heavenly realms (Eph. 3:10). He wants us to grasp this great eternal purpose and to cry out for the wisdom to understand what He's doing among us right now.

We're living in very exciting times. Never in the history of the church has there been such a worldwide anticipation of the move of God's Spirit as there is today. Past revivals tended to take people by surprise. There were usually a few individuals who knew in advance what God was going to do and who prayed faithfully for a couple of years for His intervention.

But we're seeing something totally dynamic in our time. Hundreds of thousands of Christians believe that God is going to send a mighty outpouring of His Spirit across the nations. This sense of expectancy has been around not just for a couple of years, but for twenty or thirty. It's an unprecedented move of God and it will culminate in an unparalleled manifestation of His power.

Why has God given a universal anticipation? Because He wants a universal preparation. He's not looking for demise, but for glory.

▩ To question

How can you prepare yourself for the revival to come?

____

____

What practical steps will you take now?

____

____

▩ To meditate on

We should seek wisdom.
'Wisdom is supreme; therefore get wisdom' (Prov. 4:7a).
'Solomon answered God ... "Give me wisdom and knowledge, that I may lead this people"' (2 Chr. 1:8a,10a).
'And Jesus grew in wisdom and stature' (Luke 2:52a).
'If any of you lacks wisdom, he should ask God, who gives generously to all without finding fault, and it will be given to him' (James 1:5).

One of the saddest comments on revival is this: 'The fruit doesn't last'. God comes in power and thousands are converted, but ten or fifteen years later there's almost no evidence that anything miraculous ever happened. We look back and question, 'What went wrong?' The answer is this: the wineskins couldn't hold the new wine, so they burst (Matt. 9:17a).

Only new wineskins can hold new wine. God knows that if He pours out His Spirit on old structures, they will not be able to contain His blessing. So He highlights afresh the New Testament pattern for the church, tells us what He's planning to do and urges us to get ready for it. If we're foolish, we'll do nothing; if we're wise, we'll respond.

God wants us to pray for the wisdom to build according to His plans. We must cry out to Him for our leaders — that having seen the New Testament ideal, they will understand how to apply it to the local church. We must pray too for God to raise up holy individuals — that they will be ready to disciple the hundreds of new converts. And we must act wisely ourselves. If we want God to use us in His revival, we must be diligent and get ready.

▩ To read

Read the parable of the Wise and Foolish Builders (Matt. 7:24–27).

Spend 10 minutes praying that your church leaders will have wisdom to know how to build the church.

▩ Food for thought

➢ Spend at least 30 minutes meditating on Isaiah's prayer for revival (Isa. 64).

➢ What does the prophet want God to do?

➢ Make the passage a basis for your prayers over the next couple of days.

➢ Ask God to stir your heart more for revival.

I believe the greatest revival in the history of the Church is on its way. Everywhere I go I see new, dramatic unmistakable evidence of the awesome work of preparation now being carried out by the Holy Spirit. Like a mighty tidal wave, this revival is now rising in majesty many miles from shore. Soon — only God knows when — it will come thundering inland. And in its wake, countless lives will be forever changed.
James Robison

❑ STUDY 30

There will be terrible times in the last days. People will be lovers of themselves ... lovers of pleasure rather than lovers of God — having a form of godliness but denying its power (See 2 Tim. 3:1–5).

But you are a chosen people, a royal priesthood, a holy nation, a people belonging to God, that you may declare the praises of him who called you out of darkness into his wonderful light (1 Pet. 2:9).

Pray for fruitfulness

Our churches are frequently so full of sin. We look at the established church where influential figureheads preach their own ideas, and tolerate and even encourage evil practices. And we see local congregations adopting the customs of the peoples around them and doing just about everything that unbelievers do. It often seems that there's no significant difference between those who believe in Jesus and those who don't.

We are a chosen people. God has set us apart for Himself and has given us His grace so that we can bear fruit for Him. He wants us to be 'conformed to the image of His Son' (Rom. 8:29 NASB), not to succumb to the temptation to be like everyone else around us.

How do people become Christlike? They live by the Word. While casual Christians examine the Bible, committed Christians let it examine them. They read or listen with the clear intention of aligning their lives with the truth — whether they feel like it or not.

I long to see godliness among believers — the sort of purity that was evident in the early church. Lives are changed when the Word of God touches them. The Word is described as

▩ To pray

Pray that God will raise up anointed preachers and that through them many will be saved.

When you pray, be open to being the answer to your own prayers.

Is God calling you to preach?

▩ To meditate on

Paul asked for prayer to preach.
'Pray ... for me, that whenever I open my mouth, words may be given me so that I will fearlessly make known the mystery of the gospel' (Eph. 6:19).
'Pray ... that God may open a door for our message, so that we may proclaim the mystery of Christ ... Pray that I may proclaim it clearly' (Col. 4:3,4a).
'Pray for us that the message of the Lord may spread rapidly and be honoured' (2 Thess. 3:1b).

fire, a hammer and a double-edged sword (Jer. 23:29; Heb. 4:12b). It blazes, shatters and pierces. I want to see the Word having this sort of impact in our churches today. So I pray that the Spirit will anoint biblical preaching, penetrate people's hearts and convict them 'of guilt in regard to sin and righteousness and judgment' (John 16:8).

In times of revival, God anoints certain Christians to deliver His Word with exceptional authority and power. When the apostle Peter spoke at Pentecost, 3,000 people were 'cut to the heart' and saved (Acts 2:37b,41).

David said, 'Thy people shall be willing in the day of thy power' (Ps. 110:3a AV). When God comes in power, you won't need to force people to come to the prayer meetings; they'll flood in. And you won't need to give an altar call because they'll be on their knees long before the end of the message.

If we want to see the breakthrough of the Word in the lives of individuals, we need to catch a vision for anointed powerful preaching, and to pray with the Psalmist, 'Let your sharp arrows pierce the hearts of the king's enemies; let the nations fall beneath your feet' (Ps. 45:5).

Food for thought

➢ What does it mean to be Christlike? Draw up in a notebook a list of qualities.

➢ Assess yourself in each of these areas. Where you fall short make it your goal to persist in prayer until you change.

➢ Pray for your friends and the local and national church that the Word will impact their lives and produce Christlikeness in them.

To challenge

How important is the Word of God to you?

Is it just something to read or do you live your life by it?

How would you react if you were no longer permitted to own a Bible, as was formerly the case in some Communist countries?

Only those who walk in holiness experience true joy.
Jerry Bridges

❑ **STUDY 31**

Pray for power

'Go into all the world and preach the good news to all creation ... And these signs will accompany those who believe' (Mark 16:15b,17a).

Revive us, and we will call on your name. Restore us, O LORD God Almighty; make your face shine upon us, that we may be saved (Ps. 80:18b,19).

Will you not revive us again, that your people may rejoice in you? (Ps. 85:6)

The early believers prayed, 'Lord ... enable your servants to speak your word with great boldness. Stretch out your hand to heal and perform miraculous signs and wonders' (Acts 4:29b,30a). Clearly, they expected the preaching to be accompanied by manifestations of God's power. They weren't disappointed.

Although we don't read too much about healing and miraculous signs in past revivals, there's no doubt that God moved with incredible power on the people. This happened particularly during the preaching of the Word.

Let me encourage you to read the biography of some of the great revivalists. The story of the nineteenth-century preacher, Charles Finney, has really inspired me, and his deep devotion to prayer has helped me see what incredible things can be achieved through intercession.

Finney was a lawyer in New York City. He was converted in his late twenties and when he preached, God moved in awesome power. Night after night multitudes would come to hear him. Some of them would read about him in the newspapers and turn up out of curiosity; others, like his lawyer colleagues, would be there not to listen, but to mock and heckle.

▩ To pray

Ask God to equip you with the gifts of the Spirit, especially healing and the working of miracles.

▩ To meditate on

God's glory is displayed in His wonders.
'I will gain glory through Pharaoh and all his army, through his chariots and his horsemen' (Exod. 14:17b).
'The first of his miraculous signs, Jesus performed at Cana ... He thus revealed his glory' (John 2:11a).
'Anyone who has faith in me will do what I have been doing ... I will do whatever you ask in my name, so that the Son may bring glory to the Father' (John 14:12a,13).